GET ANIMATED!

Teaching 21st Century Early Readers and Young Adult Cartoons in Language Arts

Dr. Katie Monnin

Associate Professor of Literacy, University of North Florida

Kendall Hunt
publishing company

Cover image © Shutterstock, Inc.

Kendall Hunt
publishing company

www.kendallhunt.com
Send all inquiries to:
4050 Westmark Drive
Dubuque, IA 52004-1840

Contents

About the Author

Dr. Katie Monnin is an Associate Professor of Literacy at the University of North Florida in Jacksonville, Florida. She has written four books about teaching new literacies in today's classrooms, specifically focusing on the teaching of comic books and graphic novels in K–12 education: *Teaching Graphic Novels* (2010), *Teaching Early Reader Comic Books and Graphic Novels* (2011), *Using Content-Area Graphic Texts for Learning,* co-authored with Dr. Meryl Jaffe (2012), and *Teaching Reading Comprehension with Graphic Texts* (2013). In 2013, Dr. Monnin served as a judge for San Diego Comic Con.

Chapter 1

Why Should Elementary Language Arts Educators Teach 21st Century Children's Cartoons?

"You cannot roll back the tide of social progress!"

William Seward (New York State Senator, 1850)

TEACHING 21ST CENTURY NEW LITERACIES

Personally and professionally, I relish this quote from 19th century Senator William H. Seward.

As a 21st century literacy educator it inspires me to roll with our current tide of literacy social progress and pursue a passionate and scholarly quest to help teachers implement new literacies in today's 21st century classrooms. We, the first generation of educators to ever be asked to do so, are witnesses to and participators in the most significant change in literacy history; in fact, many contemporary literacy scholars refer to it as the greatest communication revolution of all time (Buckingham, 2003; Kist, 2004, 2009; Kress, 2003; Monnin, 2010, 2011, 2012, 2013). Second on the historical time line to the 15th century invention of the printing press, our current communication revolution is more significant because it is driven by more than a single invention. Our current communication revolution is driven by an almost infinitesimal rise in 21st century new literacy advancements (the World Wide Web, text messaging, film, blogging, tweeting, television, Skype, touch screen pads, video streaming, cell phones, video games, email, and much, much more). The list could go on and on. But that's not the point. The point is that we must be aware of our own time and place in history and roll with the current tide of literacy progress. From my perspective as a contemporary literacy scholar we are fortunate. Being the first generation of teachers to embrace new literacies offers us the opportunity to lay the groundwork for generations to come. Furthermore, because we are the first generation of teachers to witness and participate in the greatest communication revolution of all-time we are transformative literacy learning change agents (Henderson & Gornik, 2007), teachers who can positively impact and influence the future of reading and writing globally.

Thus, with Senator Seward's advice in mind *Get Animated! Teaching 21st Century Early Reader and Young Adult Cartoons in Language Arts* hopes to inspire today's teachers to roll with the tide of literacy progress and teach some of the most popular, literary-level new literacies of the 21st century, like those found in children's and young adult cartoons.

EMBRACING THE 21ST CENTURY LITERACY CLIMATE

Before educators can sincerely embrace 21st century new literacies in their classrooms, such as those found in children's and young adult cartoons, I must address a reservation some readers may have. To begin, let's personally reflect on a few thought-provoking insights:

▶ Most of us grew up during a time in history when literacy-learning relied on print-text literacies alone, which makes our school experiences and schema about literacy-learning in English Language Arts outdated.
▶ Along with our students, most of us daily engage and work with new literacies.
▶ Most of us want our students to go to school in order to learn how they can be highly skilled, creative, and successful 21st century literacy citizens.
▶ In order to help our students become highly skilled, creative, and successful 21st century literacy contributors we must embrace new literacies in our classrooms.

Simply put: we must embrace the reality of the new literacy world all around us. And perhaps what is most exciting about teaching 21st century new literacies, such as those found in children's and young adult cartoons, is that we already know how to do so. The solution: pair our teaching of the standards and their emphases on reading and writing with print-text literacies to reading and writing with new literacies. Surely we will need to learn and teach some new terms. But that's just about it. Learn new terms. Pair and align them to our familiar curriculum of teaching with print-text literacies. It's a shared literacy stage. Print-text literacies and new literacies are co-stars on the modern stage of literacy education (see Figure 1.1).

Teaching new literacies with cartoons fits perfectly on the modern literacy stage, for today's cartoons pursue the same depth of storytelling we already teach with print-text literacies alone (especially in regard to the elements of story): characterization, theme, plot, setting, symbolism, rising action, climax, falling action, and much, much more. In translation, we must put on a new literacy-learning hat in order to better understand and teach high-quality 21st century new literacies. Once we understand and teach new literacies we will become the first generation of educators to respond to and impact the greatest communication revolution of all time.

FIGURE 1
The 21st century modern literacy stage equally emphasizes
teaching print-text literacies alongside visual literacies.

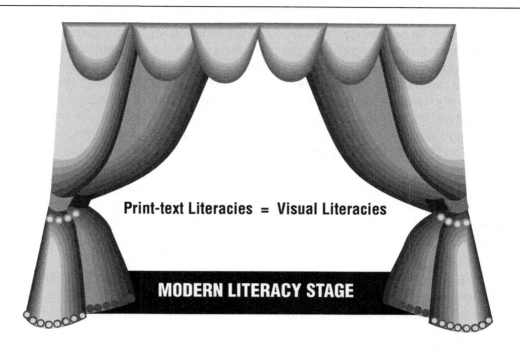

Print-text Literacies = Visual Literacies

MODERN LITERACY STAGE

HISTORICAL INSIGHTS ON WHY WE SHOULD TEACH 21ST CENTURY NEW LITERACIES

Before we can talk in greater detail about teaching cartoons in our Language Arts classrooms we must take a brief look back in time, for we cannot know where we are today unless we know where we have been—especially in the classroom.

Maybe more important than having a rationale for why today's cartoons belong in our 21st century classrooms is sharing that knowledge with colleagues, parents, administrators, and other stakeholders who may not know why cartoons are a perfect fit for contemporary, 21st century English Language Arts classrooms.

On September 11, 2001, American educators witnessed one of the most tragic and visually unexplainable events in American history. Many of these educators, myself included, did not witness these events alone. We watched them with our students.

Following the events of September 11, 2001, the literature on the importance of teaching students to comprehend what they see on-screen, both visually and textually, intensified (Buckingham, 2003; Hull & Schultz, 2002; Kist, 2004, 2009; Kress, 2003; The New London

Group, 1996). Foreseeing a shift in literacy-learning, The New London Group (1996) was the first group of scholars to explain the importance of this historical shift toward teaching visually-based screen literacies:

> Literacy pedagogy, in other words, has been a carefully restricted project . . . . What we might term "mere literacy" remains centered on language only, and usually on a singular national form of language at that, which is conceived as a stable system based on rules such as mastering sound-letter correspondence. This is based on the assumption that we can discern and describe correct usage. Such a view of language will characteristically translate into a more or less authoritarian kind of pedagogy. A pedagogy of multiliteracies, by contrast, focuses on modes of representation much broader than language alone . . . . the visual mode of representation may be much more powerful and closely related to language than "mere literacy" would ever be able to allow. (9)

Even though The New London Group's 1996 statements may seem like recent history to many of us, our modern and consistently shifting literacy climate begs us to consider time differently. In a modern literacy world the ways in which we communicate shift each and every day (Buckingham, 2003; Hobbs, 2007; Kist, 2004, 2009; Kress, 2003; The New London Group, 1996).

To help ourselves visualize the significance of our current place in history, and share it with others, we can think of a time line (Figure 1.2). On the far left of the time line is "Guttenerg's fifteenth century invention of the printing press," which made it possible for print-text literacies to be mass-produced worldwide and, therefore, raise the literacy rate around the world (causing the first global communication revolution). On the far right of the time line is "the present day." About a third of an inch to the left of the present day is the date September 11, 2001 (the demarcating date of the second, yet most significant, communication revolution). On Figure 1.2's time line we can also see that a quarter of an inch to the left of September 11, 2001, is The New London Group's 1996 article on the importance of teaching a pedagogy of multi-literacies (like those found in cartoons).

When we look at this abbreviated time line it is easier to see the progression and most important turning points toward teaching a pedagogy of multi-literacies. In fact, post-2001 the number of children's cartoons (and even cartoon channels!) has significantly increased.

Moreover, modern children's cartoons are unlike cartoons you and I may have viewed as children. Because visual literacies are so dominant in our everyday lives post-2001 the creators of modern cartoons have responded to a more intelligent viewing audience. Children's cartoons no longer start with a single event or conflict and, a half hour later, wrap it all up nice and tidy (plot point A to plot point B). Modern children's cartoons pursue the elements of story we have typically taught in English Language Arts with print-text literacies.

FIGURE 1.2
Historical overview of the two literacy communication revolutions, emphasizing the pace of our modern and visually-based communication revolution and significance.

| **15th Century** | **1996 (NLG)** | Present Day |

Figures 1.3 and 1.4 present the Common Core Standards (CCSs) for teaching reading and writing in today's Language Arts classrooms; notably evident in the new CCSs is the broad interpretation of the word "text."

FIGURE 1.3
Common Core Standards for Teaching Reading in Elementary English Language Arts Classrooms

Key Ideas and Details

1. Read closely to determine what the text says explicitly and to make logical inferences from it; cite specific textual evidence when writing or speaking to support conclusions drawn from the text.
2. Determine central ideas or themes of a text and analyze their development; summarize the key supporting details and ideas.
3. Analyze how and why individuals, events, and ideas develop and interact over the course of a text.

Craft and Structure

4. Interpret words and phrases as they are used in a text, including determining technical, connotative, and figurative meanings, and analyze how specific word choices shape meaning or tone.
5. Analyze the structure of texts, including how specific sentences, paragraphs, and larger portions of the text (e.g., a section, chapter, scene, or stanza) relate to each other and the whole.
6. Assess how point of view or purpose shapes the content and style of a text.

Integration of Knowledge and Ideas

7. Integrate and evaluate content presented in diverse media and formats, including visually and quantitatively, as well as in words.
8. Delineate and evaluate the argument and specific claims in a text, including the validity of the reasoning as well as the relevance and sufficiency of the evidence.
9. Analyze how two or more texts address similar themes or topics in order to build knowledge or to compare the approaches the authors take.

Range of Reading and Level of Text Complexity

10. Read and comprehend complex literary and informational texts independently and proficiently.*

* www.corestandards.org

FIGURE 1.4
The Common Core Standards for Teaching Writing in
Elementary English Language Arts Classrooms

Text Types and Purposes

1. Write arguments to support claims in an analysis of substantive topics or texts, using valid reasoning and relevant and sufficient evidence.
2. Write informative/explanatory texts to examine and convey complex ideas and information clearly and accurately through the effective selection, organization, and analysis of content.
3. Write narratives to develop real or imagined experiences or events using effective technique, well-chosen details, and well-structured event sequences.

Production and Distribution of Writing

4. Produce clear and coherent writing in which the development, organization, and style are appropriate to task, purpose, and audience.
5. Develop and strengthen writing as needed by planning, revising, editing, rewriting, or trying a new approach.
6. Use technology, including the Internet, to produce and publish writing and to interact and collaborate with others.

Research to Build and Present Knowledge

7. Conduct short as well as more sustained research projects based on focused questions, demonstrating understanding of the subject under investigation.
8. Gather relevant information from multiple print and digital sources, assess the credibility and accuracy of each source, and integrate the information while avoiding plagiarism.
9. Draw evidence from literary or informational texts to support analysis, reflection, and research.

Range of Writing

10. Write routinely over extended time frames (time for research, reflection, and revision) and shorter time frames (a single sitting or a day or two) for a range of tasks, purposes, and audience.*

---

* www.corestandards.org

A text is defined as any matter or format that can be communicated. Until recently we have narrowly interpreted text to mean print-text literacies alone. In fact the term stems from the 1890s Committee of Ten decision to determine what is and what is not a valid "text" in our schools' curriculums. Led by Dr. Charles Elliot, the Committee of Ten defined "text" to mean print-text literacies alone. Print-text is a matter and a format that can be communicated. It fits the definition. But so do a lot of other texts. The writers of the Common Core Standards have purposefully chosen not to specify what type of text we can and cannot teach. Fortunately, the Common Core Standards realize that the 21st century has presented us with more than one literacy learning experience that works on a literary level, and teachers are respected enough to make those decisions based upon their expertise.

Similar to the passing of the Olympic torch, the Common Core Standards have set the stage for Language Arts educators to run the next leg in the race. In this next leg of the race *Get Animated! Teaching 21st Century Early Reader and Young Adult Cartoons in Language Arts* will hopefully be one of many pieces of scholarship to carry on the idea that 21st century texts can be found in a variety of formats, one of which can be children's cartoons.

Chapter 2

Teaching Children's Cartoons in K–1st Grade Language Arts

"If you want your children to be intelligent, read them fairy tales.
If you want them to be more intelligent, read them more fairy tales."

Albert Einstein

One of the largest areas of growth in children's cartoons over the last 10 to 15 years can be found in not only the number of cartoons available for early readers in grades K–1, but also in the genesis of entire cartoon channels devoted strictly (24 hours a day!) to this viewing audience. For that reason, and coupled with our current time and place in history as literacy change agents during the greatest communication revolution of all time, it is critical that educators pay more attention to what early readers are reading and able to comprehend from the television cartoons targeted exactly at their age group.

Before we discuss these cartoons, however, let's consider Einstein's advice. For decades, it has been pretty typical for Language Arts educators to teach fairy tales and other familiar, traditional stories to early readers. Today, however, we have a new wealth of material and story to draw from. Complementing our traditional teaching of fairy tales and other familiar stories found in print-text literature are today's literary-level children's cartoons. We, my friends, are the first generation of teachers to have such a wealth of untapped literary treasure right in front of us. On television screens across the world there are an infinite amount of literary-level children's cartoons waiting to expand upon their invitation from our home television screens to our classroom television screens.

Gone are the days when it is valid to tell students: "TV isn't reading! Watch that stuff at home!" Today's cartoons are more complex and adopt all of the elements of story found in traditional print-text literature for children. In fact, the new Common Core Standards beg us to redefine what counts as literature in our early reader classrooms by purposefully and liberally using the word "texts" to refer to any contemporary format that works on a literary level to tell stories. Contemporary children's cartoons for early and young adult readers work on a literary level.

When teachers bring contemporary children's cartoons into their early reader classrooms they may be pleasantly surprised. Contemporary teachers and their young readers will find that they can learn from each other, for while students will most likely be familiar with the cartoons, teachers will most likely be familiar with pairing similar literary-level stories to the standards for teaching reading and writing in *Language Arts*. It's really an ideal classroom experience; both teachers and students can bring their schema to the table.

In this chapter of *Get Animated! Teaching 21st Century Early Reader and Young Adult Cartoons in Language Arts* educators will find the following resources for teaching 21st century cartoons alongside traditional stories to early readers in kindergarten and first grade:

▶ A reference list of cartoon channels that present modern day readers with literary level cartoons (Figure 2.1)
▶ A recommended and Common Core Standard-aligned Guided Reading lesson plan for teaching K–1 children's cartoons in Language Arts classrooms
▶ A recommended Common Core Standard-aligned writing lesson plan for teaching K–1 children's cartoons in Language Arts classrooms
▶ User-friendly versions of the suggested reading and writing lesson plans for immediate classroom use (which will be referenced in the chapter but found in the appendix)

In order to gain a clear grasp on just how literary today's early reader cartoons are, parents and teachers should spend some time watching the numerous television channels devoted to this age group (Figure 2.1).

COMMON CORE STANDARD-ALIGNED GUIDED READING LESSON PLAN FOR TEACHING K–1 CHILDREN'S CARTOONS IN LANGUAGE ARTS

Guided Reading (Fountas & Pinnell, 1996) is a very user-friendly methodological approach for teaching children's cartoons in kindergarten and first grade Language Arts classrooms. With only three steps—Before Reading, During Reading, and After Reading—its format is simple. Umbrellaed by a three-step structure, teachers can think about planning each step as its own mini-lesson (a total of three mini-lessons), each mini-lesson appropriate to its order in the lineup. The Before Reading mini-lesson builds schema and introduces the new material. The During Reading mini-lesson calls on teachers to focus on identifying the elements of story (plot, setting, characters, rising action, climax, falling action, themes, symbols, and so on). Finally, the After Reading mini-lesson reviews and assesses student comprehension.

For this particular reading-focused lesson we will work through all three of the Guided Reading steps (see Figure 2.2). Note: Even though the following suggested Guided Reading Lesson Plan specifically mentions the cartoon *Arthur* from ABC Kids channel, teachers can find a blank, user-friendly lesson plan in the Appendix for their own cartoon choices (Appendix A).

FIGURE 2.1

Television channels appropriate for kindergarten and first grade
Language Arts classrooms and above.

Television Channels Devoted To Kindergarten and First Grade Readers
Boomerang www.boomerangtv.co.uk
Cartoon Network www.cartoonnetwork.com
Disney www.disney.com
Disney Junior www.disney.go.com/disneyjunior
ABC Kids TV http://www.abc.net.au/abcforkids/
Disney XD www.disney.go.com/disneyxd/
National Geographic Kids http://www.tv.com/shows/national-geographic-channel-kids/
Nickelodeon www.nick.com
Nick Jr. www.nickjr.com
NickToons Kids Live! www.livestream.com/cartoonnetworkhubnicktoons
PBS Kids www.pbskids.org
Smile of a Child www.smileofachild.org
Sprout www.sproutonline.com
Zoo Live TV http://fancystreems.com/zoo-live-kids-channel.php

FIGURE 2.2
Guided Reading lesson plan for teaching children's cartoons in
K–1st Grade Language Arts classrooms (Appendix A).

YOU WILL NEED THE FOLLOWING MATERIALS FOR THIS LESSON PLAN:

▶ projection screen/television
▶ the cartoon episode of your choice, which can be found online through the network's cartoon listings, or online at youtube.com
▶ blank paper
▶ crayons, markers, pencils, colored pencils, and pens

COMMON CORE STANDARD ALIGNMENT

Key Ideas and Details

1. Read closely to determine what the text says explicitly and to make logical inferences from it; cite specific textual evidence when writing or speaking to support conclusions drawn from the text.
2. Determine central ideas or themes of a text and analyze their development; summarize the key supporting details and ideas.
3. Analyze how and why individuals, events, and ideas develop and interact over the course of a text.

COMMON CORE STANDARD-ALIGNED WRITING LESSON PLAN FOR TEACHING K–1 CHILDREN'S CARTOONS IN LANGUAGE ARTS CLASSROOMS

Equally important as teaching children how to read literary-level children's cartoons is teaching children how to write their own literary-level children's cartoons; after all, the readers of the present will become the writers of the future. For that reason, the following lesson plan focuses on aligning the Common Core Standards for writing to teaching K–1st grade literary-level children's cartoon (Figure 2.3). A blank, classroom-friendly, and adaptable version for this K–1st grade lesson plan for teaching writing with children's cartoons can be found in the back of the book, Appendix B.

Before Reading

Arthur—Season: 16—Episode: 5b—"Read and Flumberghast"

http://www.youtube.com/watch?v=_818bVDw038

Before reading ask students what they **KNOW** either about Arthur and/or the idea of imagination. Next, ask students what they **WONDER** either about Arthur or imagination. On the board, record their responses in the appropriate **KNOW-and-WONDER** categories.

KNOW	WONDER

During Reading

As students read and view this episode about Arthur and imagination, pause the episode at least three times. During each pause ask students what they have **LEARNED** about Arthur and his friends. On the board teachers can visually emphasize and honor student responses by adding, and keeping notes on a third category of discussion (**LEARN**).

KNOW	WONDER	LEARN

After Reading

When students are done viewing and reading, it's time to check-in on their overall comprehension of this particular episode of Arthur. To do so, teachers can ask their students to be cartoonists themselves. Allow students to choose one of the following two prompts; due to the early grade level of these students, I recommend reading each prompt aloud and making sure it is also visible somewhere else in the room.

"On your paper, draw a picture of your **favorite Arthur character**. What does this character look like? What do we know about him or her? How does what you drew reflect this character's personality? After you finish drawing be ready to share your drawing with the class."

or

"On your paper, write down some words or images that help you remember the most important **character or characters** from this episode."

FIGURE 2.3
Common Core standard-aligned lesson plan for teaching writing with K–1st grade children's cartoons.

Directions

1. Before watching an episode of *Dora the Explorer* display a large cut-out image of Dora for all students to see. In order to build upon their already existing or new schema, ask students to share what they already know about Dora. Draw images or write words to represent all of the various ideas students have about Dora.
2. Next, tell students: "As we watch this episode of *Dora the Explorer* pretend you are a detective. A detective looks for clues about people, places, and/or ideas. When you are done watching the episode, we will discuss our findings."
3. Before you finally turn on the episode ask students if they have any questions. Next, play the selected episode of *Dora the Explorer.*
4. When the episode is over write the following key words from the directions on the board, near the image of Dora: "detective," "Dora," "friends," and "events." Remind students about the definitions for each key word.
5. After reminding them about each word, ask students to recall—with words and images—what they learned from watching this episode, especially in terms of Dora, her friends, and the events in the story. Discuss the student's writing and/or drawing suggestions as you move from one response to the next response.

When students are able to identify reading and writing tasks in K–1st grade Language Arts classrooms, they are setting up the groundwork to be successful literacy learners in the 21st century, for they are prepared to read and to write with both words and images. In the next chapter, we will build upon this foundation and alignment to the Common Core Standards by exploring two more—intensified—reading and writing lesson plans with children's cartoons in third and fourth grade Language Arts classrooms.

Chapter 3

Teaching Children's Cartoons in 2nd–3rd Grade Language Arts

Whenever I visit second and third grade classrooms students are quick to tell me about everything they are interested in: hobbies, sports, favorite TV shows, favorite films, favorite cereals, vacations, and much, much more. Lately, the second and third graders have been telling me a lot about their favorite cartoons. And, without fail, their passionate interest and wealth of information about each cartoon spurs on a Peter Pan-ish Lost Boys daydream-trip where I try extra-hard to will myself to be a kid again. Intrusive yet sincere, my adult mind plays detective in order to enter their world. Sometimes I imagine thought balloons appearing above their heads, testing my sincerity: *Does she* **REALLY** *watch this? Or is she tricking us, like Captain Hook?*

Full of detail, and all of the elements of story that make traditional children's literature ageless and beyond beauty, what the kids don't know and I do know is that my secret ambition has always been to be "Professor Peter Pan," a kid who had to grow up and was forced to physically look like an adult (although that is sometimes in debate if you know me). As a result, I have spent my adult years studying and following modern children's cartoons and how they do indeed literarily stand up alongside traditional children's literature.

My graduate in-service and undergraduate pre-service students are notorious for quoting me as saying: "Kids are smarter than adults!" It's true. They are explorers of life and of literacy, and they have yet to be constrained by societal norms that tell them picture books and visual literacies are only intended for them to grow out of and leave behind. The seemingly-inevitable assumption that "real reading" only takes place when reading a print-text book with no pictures typically takes place at this critical grade and age level. Traditionally, our null curriculum has stated that print-text reading alone is intelligent and image-based reading needs to be left behind in order to enhance intelligent, intellectual reading in the upper grade levels. In the 21st century, this is completely not true!

Thirty years after Gardner's (1983) *Frames of Mind* pointed out that each individual learner has his or her own unique intelligence(s) (aka: multiple intelligences) educators still seem to emphasize print-text literacies above all other literacy intelligences, especially as second and third grade students prepare for their upper elementary fourth, fifth, and sixth grade classroom futures. For that reason, second and third grade Language Arts teachers have a new responsibility. A new responsibility to set the stage for generations to come. Embracing our current communication revolution and its emphasis on teaching both print-text and visual-text literacies, second and third grade teachers must switch gears and carry a very heavy yet exciting responsibility to teach multiple literacies in 21st century classrooms (The New London Group, 1996). Because they rely on both print-text and image-text to tell a story, children's cartoons are a perfect fit. Applicable to the Common Core Standards for reading and writing in second and third grade Language Arts classrooms, these children's cartoons provide the perfect platform for today's second and third grade teachers to step up to the plate and present a just and equal emphasis on reading multiple literacies.

The Common Core Standards' focus on the craft and structure of a story are an ideal place for second and third grade teachers to start (see Figure 3.1).

With the craft and structure of children's cartoons at the forefront of our minds, this chapter of *Get Animated: Teaching 21st Century Early Reader and Young Adult Cartoons in Language Arts* presents the following resources for teaching 21st century cartoons in second and third grade Language Arts classrooms:

▶ A reference list of specific cartoons appropriate for second and third grade readers (Figure 3.2)
▶ A recommended and Common Core Standard-aligned reading lesson plan for teaching children's cartoons in Language Arts classrooms
▶ Two recommended Common Core Standard-aligned writing lesson plan for teaching children's cartoons in Language Arts classrooms
▶ Teacher-friendly versions of the suggested reading and writing lesson plans for immediate classroom use (which will be referenced in the chapter but found in the appendix)

FIGURE 3.1
The Common Core Standards' focus on craft and structure for second and third grade Language Arts students.

Common Core Standard for Teaching Children's Cartoons in Second and Third Grade Language Arts Classrooms

Craft and Structure

1. Interpret words and phrases as they are used in a text, including determining technical, connotative, and figurative meanings, and analyze how specific word choices shape meaning or tone.
2. Analyze the structure of texts, including how specific sentences, paragraphs, and larger portions of the text (e.g., a section, chapter, scene, or stanza) relate to each other and the whole.
3. Assess how point of view or purpose shapes the content and style of a text.*

FIGURE 3.2
Reference list of high-quality children's cartoons applicable to second and third grade Language Arts classrooms.

Cartoon and Channel	Brief Description
Lego Ninjago Masters of Spinjitzu Cartoon Network	Young ninjas strive to become masters of Spinjitzu. Before they can reach their goal, however, they must learn to work as a team and figure out how each of their own unique skills will make the team stronger.
Amazing World of Gumball Cartoon Network	Gumball is the oldest child of Mr. and Mrs. Watterson, an eccentric couple perfectly paired due to their hilarious co-dependence on each other's strengths and weaknesses. Anais and—the audience is encouraged to mysteriously assume—Darwin are Gumball's adventurous siblings.
Yu-Gi-Oh Nicktoons	As a young adult who must figure out his place in the world, alongside being handed an ancient Egyptian Artifact ("The Millennium Puzzle") by his grandfather, Yu-Gi Mutuo finds himself a slightly shorter than average high school student. Thinking about his life and the world around him he begins to reassemble the artifact/puzzle and finds it possessed by a 3,000-year-old Pharaoh named Atem. The foundational story set, teachers will find a plethora of *Yu-Gi-Oh* episodes to bring into their classrooms, both on television and on DVD.
Scooby-Doo Cartoon Network	Reinvented for an entirely new generation of young readers and writers the "Clue Crew" is at it again, solving mysteries and using all of their updated gadgets to do so: text messaging, wireless internet, infrared spy gear, night vision, and much, much more.
Ben 10 Cartoon Network	Created by the geniuses at Man of Action (including the brilliant writer of both cartoons and graphic novels Joe Kelly), this cartoon focuses on a young boy with an extremely unique watch. With villainous aliens poised to take over the world, young Ben 10 must use his watch to find the right superhero good-guy combination to match and beat his opponents.
Gravity Falls Disney	Clever and endearing, the two main characters in this cartoon are forced to spend their summer with their awkwardly weird uncle, "Grumple Stan," who owns The Mystery Shack. A tourist-trap stocked full of Gravity Falls' most eccentric oddities and unexplainable finds Grumple Stan is a thought-provoking character the children come to adore. And that's where their adventures begin.

FIGURE 3.2
Continued.

Cartoon and Channel	Brief Description
Curious George PBS	The man in the yellow hat and his adorable monkey Curious George have stood the test of time. For generations they have entertained us with all of George's curiosities and the adventures that stem from them.
Spongebob Squarepants Nicktoons	Probably the most resilient cartoon over the last ten years *Spongebob Squarepants* has proven to viewers that he and his friends can tell many high-quality stories about a personified sponge who lives at the bottom of the ocean in a pineapple house, next door to his best friend Patrick, and his other next door and cranky neighbor Squidward. Their stories take them beyond their residential homes, however, as Squidward and Spongebob work at Mr. Crab's restaurant, The Crusty Crab, together and Spongebob is a very active and excitable resident of Bikini Bottom.
Arthur PBS	Based on the children's picture book by Marc Brown, the children's *Arthur* cartoon first debuted in 1996. The series follows Arthur and his friends as they face day-to-day real life issues faced by kids every single day.
Phineas and Ferb Disney	Extremely popular and adored by kids and adults alike, *Phineas and Ferb* centers on the 104 days between the end of one school year and the beginning of the next: summer vacation. Two highly intelligent and mechanically-inclined grade school brothers can dream and create anything they think of, each and every single day of their summer vacation. That is, unless their nosey sister Candice doesn't tell on them first.

Even though these are some of the most popular cartoons being taught in second and third grade Language Arts classrooms teachers should feel encouraged to view and consider the plethora of other cartoons being produced as well. Significant reading and writing lesson plan opportunities are embedded in many of their story lines. For the purposes of this chapter, however, *Get Animated! Teaching 21st Century Early Reader and Young Adult Cartoons in Language Arts* will focus on one enormously successful and clever cartoon.

TEACHING CRAFT AND STRUCTURE IN SECOND AND THIRD GRADE LANGUAGE ARTS

Phineas and Ferb first officially aired in February of 2008. An extremely thoughtful and well-plotted story it was an immediate success. Gaining even more popularity from year-to-year, *Phineas and Ferb* centers on the imaginations and insanely brilliant capabilities of two young brothers as they dream of building, creating, and/or making something new each and every day of their summer vacation. Not without some tension *Phineas and Ferb* also has three other main characters: Phineas and Ferb's older sister Candice, Dr. Doffenschmirtz, and Perry the Platypus. While Candice seeks out any opportunity to get the boys in trouble for their outlandish and sometimes hysterical inventions, Dr. Doffenschmirtz is an evil villain paired up with what appears to be Phineas and Ferb's family pet, Perry the Platypus. Not your ordinary family pet—and it's not because he's a platypus!—Perry is a secret agent who rivals the boys in order to save the day during each episode.

With its rich plot to start from *Phineas and Ferb* easily aligns to the Common Core Standards for teaching reading craft and structure in second and third grade Language Arts. By interpreting both the images and the words used to tell the story, students can be asked to analyze and critique the plot and its characters, ultimately assessing how each individual character's point of view informs his/her perspective on what "really" happened during the episode (refer to Figure 3.1). Figure 3.3 offers one example lesson plan for teaching reading craft and structure with *Phineas and Ferb;* Appendix C presents the same lesson plan, but is a blank and teacher-friendly version for teachers to use with any cartoon of their choice.

Finally, after students have recorded their responses ask them to once again meet in their groups and discuss each character and what they wrote or drew about that character. After five–seven minutes, students can return to their original (first) poster station. This time, however, they will add all of their new knowledge about the characters and how each character relates to their characterization, setting(s), plot(s), theme(s), and point of view(s).

With this last step complete, teachers can once again bring the poster boards to the front of the room and engage the entire class in an analysis of each crafted element of story and how it informs the entire story and the characters' various points of view.

TEACHING WRITING WITH CHILDREN'S CARTOONS IN SECOND AND THIRD GRADE LANGUAGE ARTS CLASSROOMS

Perhaps even more thrilling than choosing one of their favorite cartoons to teach 21st century reading skills is offering students a chance to write their own, unique cartoon episodes. With so many engaging plot points through which to view *Phineas and Ferb*, for instance, teachers can easily apply the Common Core Standards for teaching writing in second and third grade Language Arts (see Figure 3.4) to any single episode. A blank, teacher-friendly version of this writing lesson plan for second and third grade Language Arts students can be found in Appendix D.

FIGURE 3.3
A carousel reading lesson plan for teaching the Common Core Standard's emphasis on craft and structure in second and third grade Language Arts classrooms.

Three-Step Reading Carousel Activity for Teaching The Common Core Standards' Focus on Craft and Structure in Second and Third Grade Language Arts with Disney's *Phineas And Ferb*

Step 1: Schema Building

Before students enter the classroom and are ready to start their day post five stations around the room: labeled "character(s)," "setting(s)," "plot(s)," "theme(s)," and point of view(s)." In case students need some help building schema about any of these structural and craft-oriented terms please feel free to add helpful definitions below their labels.

As they enter the classroom inform them that they will be rotating like a carousel—clockwise—in small groups of three to five.

In small groups ask students to report to one of the five stations displayed throughout the room.

The directions on the board should read: "There are five stations around the room. We will work through the stations two different times, **once before reading and once after reading.**

To start, we will activate our schema about some key terms found in crafting high-quality stories, emphasizing important components such as character(s), setting(s), plot(s), theme(s), and point of view(s)."

Teacher Notes: Please be sure to put your station-postings around the room on large, visible paper. For upcoming student usage you will also want to leave a few writing utensils at each station as well.

Your next set of directions for students should read like this: "Each station is labeled and contains a critical element of story term. And even though I have provided you with brief definitions please use the markers at each station to come up with your own ideas/your own words to define each term during our first carousel session. You can write your ideas directly on the poster board."

After giving each group 10 minutes at each station, take the poster boards down and bring them to the front of the room, for a full classroom discussion of what each group wrote down for each term.

(Continued)

Step 2: Empowering Students to Know the Significant 21st Century Literacies of Their Own Time and Place in History

Before completing step number 2, educators will want to show their students an episode of *Phineas and Ferb*. That said, and from someone who adores children and is a fan of the show herself, any episode you select will be of high quality.

Before turning the episode on remind students that:

"You are the first, most unique and exciting generation to ever experience the vast amount of changes currently happening all around the world in regard to reading and writing; indeed, you are the very first students to set the stage for reading and writing with multiple literacies for generations to come. That's a pretty awesome superhero responsibility. Right now—today—is an opportunity to make a significant and critical difference in not only the future of reading for yourselves, but also the future of reading for your own future children.

Capable of determining what it means to read from instantaneous access to a variety of screen-like and image-dominant 21st century platforms, your generation reads multiple literacies every day: especially from RPG and educational videogames, iPads, iPhones, text messaging, Skype, internet, and emails, you are in written and visual contact with anyone in the world at any time of day or night."

With their empowered and special hero-like qualities at the forefront as motivation, it is now time to watch the selected episode of *Phineas and Ferb*.

Step 3: Building a New Literacy Bridge

Because our students are living during a critical time in history, and we are teaching them during that time (an age-level when previous generations of our colleagues have been encouraged to steer children away from visuals and toward an emphasis on print-text literacies alone) this third step is critical to teaching a shared literacy stage with two actors upon it: image text and verbal text.

For that reason, the third step in this reading lesson for second and third grade readers of children's cartoons asks students to think about both the visuals and the words that inform each of the previously mentioned crafted elements of story: plot, character, theme, setting, and point of view.

As they read the episode ask students to complete the following worksheet.

Directions: To the right of each character, list or draw the words and the images that give this character his/her unique perspective about what happens in this episode.

	Words	/	Images
Phineas			
Ferb			
Candice			
Perry			
Dr. Doffenschmirtz			

FIGURE 3.4
Common Core Standard alignment for teaching writing with *Phineas and Ferb*
to second and third grade Language Arts students.

Text Types and Purposes

1. Write arguments to support claims in an analysis of substantive topics or texts, using valid reasoning and relevant and sufficient evidence.
2. Write informative/explanatory texts to examine and convey complex ideas and information clearly and accurately through the effective selection, organization, and analysis of content.
3. Write narratives to develop real or imagined experiences or events using effective technique, well-chosen details, and well-structured event sequences.

Displaying the completed and discussed poster paper from the reading lesson teachers can begin the writing lesson by maintaining the carousel of stations around the room. Again in small groups, ask students to report to one of the stations. Figure 3.5 offers directions and key Common Core Standard alignment terminology for teaching students to write their own cartoon episode of *Phineas and Ferb*.

When students have completed writing their own, new episodes of *Phineas and Ferb* teachers may want to offer them extra time to act out their new episode idea. Like Reader's Theatre, students would engage in a second writing stage that asks them to focus on the next set of key Common Core Standards for writing in second and third grade Language Arts. Figure 3.6 highlights the Common Core Standards students would be working with if allowed time to complete this extra, supplemental writing activity focused on children's cartoons.

Because they are writing for a specific task—to perform their new episodes of *Phineas and Ferb*—to a specific audience of their peers students will need to be cognizant of their new episode's clarity and coherency. Essentially, their goal is to make it easy for their peers to believe that this could really be an actual episode of *Phineas and Ferb;* their focus on characters, themes, plots, and point of views need to be realistic and believable. If they are successful in doing so, teachers can use their new written and performed episode as an assessment tool for making sure students comprehended the Common Core Standards' focus on text type and purpose.

With so much creative reading and writing work already completed, these future fourth and fifth grade students can look forward to even more exciting opportunities and advanced lessons about reading and writing with their favorite cartoons in fourth and fifth grade Language Arts.

FIGURE 3.5
Directions and Common Core Standard alignment for teaching second and third grade students to write their own *Phineas and Ferb* episode. In the Appendices at the end of the book, teachers can find a blank, user-friendly version of this lesson plan and its directions (Appendix D).

DIRECTIONS

Step 1:

With your group members, report to one of the carousel stations around the room. One group per station.

Step 2:

Once at your station take note of the category you will be focusing on and review the work the class recently completed about that particular category during the reading lesson plan.

Step 3:

Please note that another, second blank piece of poster paper is also now hanging at this station, complete with the corresponding categorical label.

Step 4:

After reviewing the reading lesson plan work you previously engaged in for each category discuss some new ideas centered on your assigned category. For example, if your category is "plot" brainstorm some new "plot" ideas for a potential, future episode of *Phineas and Ferb*.

Your new ideas need to focus on two criteria:

1. A realistic portrayal of what we learned about your category given the previous episode. The "theme" group, for instance, will want to make sure that their ideas about the themes are accurate and reflective of what we already know, and
2. Strong emphasis on further developing your assigned category as the main subject for a new story idea (for instance, the characters group will want to center their new episode ideas on character development).

Continued.

FIGURE 3.5
Continued.

Step 5:

With your group's categorical emphasis at the center of your discussion work together to write your own episode of *Phineas and Ferb*. You will have between 30 and 45 minutes to outline or write out your ideas.

Step 6:

Present your ideas to the rest of the class in the following order:

1. Identify your category.
2. Share your new episode idea, particularly how you will further explore your assigned category.
3. Explain and answer peer's questions about how your new idea emphasizes the category you were assigned and a further, growing knowledge of a character(s).

Potential Starter-Questions to Ask Each Group:

▶ "Why did you decide to . . .?"
▶ "What was your goal in choosing to . . .?"
▶ "Who came up with the idea to _____, and how did the idea build?"
▶ "How did your group work together to reach the decision to . . .?"

FIGURE 3.6
Common Core Standard alignment for a supplemental, extra writing activity regarding teaching *Phineas and Ferb* in second and third grade Language Arts (Appendix E).

Production and Distribution of Writing

1. Produce clear and coherent writing in which the development, organization, and style are appropriate to task, purpose, and audience.

Chapter 4

Teaching Children's Cartoons in 4th–5th Grade Language Arts

"I like physics, but I love cartoons."

Stephen Hawking

On September 11, 2001, at 8:30 a.m. I took my first sip of morning coffee. And as I finished I began to relate the day's agenda to my upper elementary students. As they politely listened an unexpected knock was heard at the door.

This was not your ordinary knock. It was different. It was heavy, serious "thud-Thud-THUD!"

Before I could get there my principal opened the door and ran into the room. She took a beeline straight for me. As she got closer she cupped her hands and whispered in my ear: "A national emergency has happened at the Trade Center buildings. Turn on the TV and talk to the kids." Just as quickly she ran out, slamming the door behind her.

I could immediately feel the heaviness of the moment. I put down my coffee; I didn't need it anymore, and for some reason my body knew that. I walked to the back corner of the room to turn on the television. While walking I informed the kids that our schedule might be different today and that we would turn on the TV and listen so we could better understand a "national emergency" currently occurring. The kids quieted down, eerily almost, their pin-drop silence foreshadowing the unexplainable and shocking images we were about to see and always remember.

Being vertically challenged I had to stand on a chair to turn on the television. After hitting the power button, the screen blinking on, the second plane hit the World Trade Center building in live time. With smoke billowing out of both Trade Center buildings now, my upper level grade school students reacted with confusion. While one student began to cry (he knew the World Trade Center buildings because his dad had shown him pictures of where he would be traveling that week), another student stood up and shouted, "Sweet movie! That's the best movie explosion I've ever seen!"

These two reactions changed my life. In that instant I knew what I wanted to do with the rest of my life, especially for this critical age of readers, children quickly moving from childhood toward young adulthood. In hindsight, a virtual thought balloon must have appeared above my head: "They don't know how to read what they see. The images."

It is every 21st century educator's responsibility (Buckingham, 2003; Hobbs, 1998, 2007; Gee, 2003; Kist, 2004, 2009; Kress, 2003; Monnin, 2010, 2011, 2012, 2013; The New London Group, 1996) to understand and come to terms with the fact that today's 21st century upper elementary students are an entirely new set of readers. They have been raised reading both images and words, often from screen or screen-like environments. Laptops and PCs. Television. iPads. Cell phones. Panel-by-panel screen shots used in comics and graphic novels.

In a critical study based on identifying this age level's reading and writing abilities, Hull and Schultz (2002) *School's out: Bridging in-and-out-of school literacies* tracked upper elementary grade school students whenever they engaged in reading and writing activities (at school and at home). The results: kids who were labeled as poor readers and writers in school were prolific readers and writers outside of school, at home. The reason: upper elementary schools were judging and placing value on students' print-text literacy learning skills alone. In a modern era where reading and writing takes place in a variety of formats, especially those found on screen-like environments, kids are smarter than we realize. They are reading and writing in a variety of manners and doing so in an extremely intelligent and proficient manner with the words and images that compose their 21st century literacy lives.

In order to reach out to this critical generation and grade level population of readers, educators need to continue placing value on a more visual literacy learning world. To do so, Figure 4.1 offers teachers a list of some of the most long-standing and contemporarily popular cartoons appropriate for grades four and five.

For the purpose of this chapter of *Get Animated!: Teaching 21st Century Early Reader and Young Adult Cartoons Language Arts* this chapter will focus on the cartoon *Avatar: The Last Airbender*. Originally aired from 2005–2008 *Avatar: The Last Airbender* was the first cartoon to garner literary acclaim for fourth grade readers and above. Composed like a print-text book each series of the cartoon is an individual book: "Book One," Book Two," and "Book Three." Likewise, each episode of the series is referred to as a "chapter." For these reasons, and its complexity and depth of storytelling, *Avatar the Last Airbender* caught many of us by surprise. Teachers around the world seemed to think: "A cartoon formatted as a book? Really?" And when we went to watch it the answer was: "Yes, really!"

As mentioned in earlier chapters, with the new Common Core Standards teachers can use complex, literary-level cartoons in their classrooms. Even with older students who are quickly approaching junior high. In fact, fourth and fifth grade students are the perfect audience for this cartoon. At these grade levels students are able to and interested in identifying and explaining the purpose behind reading a specific text in a specific format. Building upon that schema, then, teachers can pair student schema with a more in-depth reading and writing lesson plan focused on the Common Core Standards emphasis on integration and ideas between multiple texts (Figure 4.2).

FIGURE 4.1
Cartoons applicable to the Common Core Standards for teaching reading and writing in fourth and fifth grade.

Cartoon and Channel	Brief Description
Clone Wars Cartoon Network (available for download, and on DVD & Blu-Rray)	Continuing the ageless and timeless storytelling that attracted us as young readers, this series focuses on the Clone Wars, which took place as Anakin Skywalker came of age as a young Jedi, under the Master Jedi counsel of Obi Wan Kenobi.
Ultimate Spider-Man Disney (available for download and on DVD)	Created by the always ingenious minds at Man of Action today's young readers get an all-new look at Peter Parker and Spiderman. Talking to the reader as if he or she were his diary, Peter Parker narrates his adventures in this all-new series. Complete with 21st century gadgets, lingo, and themes readers and teachers will both be able to explore how Spiderman presents himself to 21st century viewers.
New Looney Tunes Show Cartoon Network (available for download)	My favorite new young adult cartoon show, the beloved Warner Brother's *Looney Tunes* has been remastered for the 21st century viewer. Starring Bugs and Daffy as two bachelors who live in a suburban neighborhood, on a busy cul de sac of course, this series breathes new and hilarious life into a classic cartoon franchise. Bugs (the inventor of the carrot peeler lives nicely off his royalties) and Daffy (a self-consumed yet charming and arrogant friend of Bugs who lives well off his best friend's' generosity) this series focuses on the development of old characters (including Speedy and Porky) and new characters. Clever and laugh out loud funny, the new and old characters combine for an all-new sure to be classic and funny cartoon. Similar to how we reminisce about the older *The Looney Tunes,* today's young readers will tell their children about this new *Looney Tunes* series.
Slugterra Disney (available for download)	The world of Slugterra is in desperate need of a hero, and Eli Shane just may be that hero. Following in his father's legacy, Eli Shane and the Shane gang (along with their friendly slugs) will protect Slugterra from the evils that threaten it. Key to this new series is lightning fast action sequences and super-cool, creative weaponry.

FIGURE 4.1
Continued.

Cartoon and Channel	Brief Description
Randy Cunningham: 9th Grade Ninja Disney (available for download)	Unknown to the citizens of Norrisville their town is guarded by an 800-year-old Ninja tradition. Every four years the town of Norrisville is secretly assigned a guardian Ninja. At the beginning of his high school career, and in parallel with the Ninja tradition, Randy Cunningham is not only a new ninth grade student in high school, but also the next guardian Ninja of Norrisville. Juggling his new high school status with his secret identity Randy's dualistic roles make this new series worthy of much more classroom discussion.
Invader Zim Cartoon Network (available on DVD)	Available on DVD, this series maintains its status as one of the best cartoons of the 21st century. Intended for a young adult viewership Invader Zim is like any other alien character, right? He's out to take over the world! That's what Zim thinks, and he'll tell you too. It's not necessarily what his leaders or his earthly nemesis Dib think about the situation. Zim is a terrible and clumsy alien who trips all over what he thinks are his brilliant plans to destroy the world. Witty and sharp, Zim and his hilarious sidekick Gir maintain a loyal following.
Regular Show Cartoon Network (available for download, and on DVD and Blu-ray)	Another show best introduced to fourth grade viewers and above Regular Show is a new hit cartoon that first aired in 2010. Centered on bachelors Mordecai and Rigby—two twenty-three-year-old bachelors—this cartoon features a number of noteworthy characters who are now appearing on t-shirts, backpacks, and as action figures this cartoon takes place in "The Park." Living in the park's guest house and working in the park Mordecai and Rigby really want to keep their jobs. But they have a tendency to accidentally (maybe purposefully) get into trouble. Join the pair as they work and live together with their unforgettable co-stars: Muscle Man, Skips, Benson, Pops, and more.
LEGO Ninjago: Masters of Spinjitsu Cartoon Network (available for download and on DVD)	Applicable to fourth and fifth grade readers and younger readers (as mentioned in Chapter 3) this cartoon spotlights four young ninjas as they strive to become masters of Spinjitsu. Before they can reach their goal, however, they must learn to work as a team and figure out how each of their own unique skills will make the team stronger.

FIGURE 4.1
Continued.

Cartoon and Channel	Brief Description
Avatar: The Last Airbender Nickelodeon (available on DVD)	Already a legend and also frequently referred to as one of the best cartoons in the last decade, *Avatar: The Last Airbender* is a literary treasure trove for teachers and students to discover. Formatted to mimic a chapter book series each series is referred to as a "Book" ("Book One," "Book Two," and so on) and each episode a chapter in that book. Key to the plot, readers follow young Aang as he and his friends must figure out where they fit in an Asian-influenced world that still believes in the ancient and spiritual powers of a psychokinetic art format called "bending." The characters must ask themselves: "Am I an air bender? A water bender? A fire bender? Or an earth bender?" And depending on that answer, "How can I help fight against the evil, destructive, and aggressive rule of the fire nation?"
Beyblade Cartoon Network (available on DVD and Blu-ray)	Written in response to the enormous popularity of the spinning-top toys called "Beyblades," this series centers on various teams of Beybladers. Each team competes to see who has the most powerful and most engaging Beyblade techniques and skills. Themes such as team play, individuality, friendship, rivalry, and action are ripe for classroom discussion.

FIGURE 4.2
Teaching the Common Core Standard's emphasis on Integration of Knowledge and Ideas in fourth and fifth grade Language Arts classrooms.

Common Core Standard Alignment for Teaching Children's Cartoons in Fourth and Fifth Grade Language Arts Classrooms

Integration of Knowledge and Ideas

1. Integrate and evaluate content presented in diverse media and formats, including visually and quantitatively, as well as in words.
2. Delineate and evaluate the argument and specific claims in a text, including the validity of the reasoning as well as the relevance and sufficiency of the evidence.
3. Analyze how two or more texts address similar themes or topics in order to build knowledge or to compare the approaches the authors take.

Even though these are some of the more advanced Common Core Standards for teaching reading in K–5 classrooms, pairing an animated cartoon with a print-text book is a perfect and simple solution. In regard to pairing, *Get Animated!: Teaching 21st Century Early Reader and Young Adult Cartoons Language Arts* recommends one of two possible pairings when teaching Elementary Language Arts with *Avatar: The Last Airbender*:

1. Due to its popularity teachers can easily find both print-text books and/or graphic novels to pair with the *Avatar* cartoon.
2. Due to its timelessness and high quality storytelling teachers can also easily choose a more traditional fourth or fifth grade print-text book to pair with *Avatar*.

Some of the most recognizable and thematically similar fourth and fifth grade chapter books teachers may want to consider are:

▶ *Harry Potter and the Sorcerer's Stone* by J.K. Rowling
▶ *Holes* by Louis Sachar
▶ *Hatchet* by Gary Paulsen
▶ *Walk Two Moons* by Sharon Creech
▶ *The Secret Garden* by Frances Hodgson Burnett
▶ *Charlotte's Web* by E.B. White
▶ *Esperanza Rising* by Pam Munoz Ryan
▶ *The Tale of Despereaux* or *Because of Winn Dixie* by Kate DiCamillo
▶ *The Trouble with May Amelia* by Jennifer L. Holm
▶ *Where the Mountain Meets the Moon* by Grace Lin

Paired with either a thematically similar print-text novel or a graphic novel teachers are now ready to plan their reading lesson (Figure 4.3). Teachers can find a blank, user-friendly, and adaptable version of this lesson plan in Appendix F.

With the reading lesson plan handouts completed and collected teachers can begin to think about a writing lesson plan based on *Avatar* (or any cartoon of their choice) and *Walk Two Moons* (or any print-text book of their choice). Connecting their work on the reading of *Walk Two Moons* and *Avatar* teachers can begin by returning the two KWL handouts to students. After doing so, ask students to review their ideas in small groups.

With a little bit of preparation teachers can turn toward writing with a very exciting, game-like writing activity. In order to do so, and previous to handing back the two KWL handouts, teachers need to prepare the following materials:

1. 80 index cards: Teachers will want to prepare two sets of 40 index cards, one set for the cartoon and one set for the print-text novel.
2. On these two sets of 40 index cards (total of 80) pull out 10 of the best student answers or ideas about what students learned in regard to the four main categories of plot, setting, characters, and favorite moments (during the reading lesson plan). With a marker, have those ideas written down on the index cards and separate them into eight piles: four for the *Avatar* handout (setting, plot, characters, favorite moments) and four for *Walk Two Moons* (setting, plot, characters, favorite moments).

FIGURE 4.3
Teaching reading with children's cartoons in 21st century
fourth and fifth grade Language Arts classrooms.

Teaching Reading with Children's Cartoons in Fourth and Fifth Grade 21st Century Language Arts Classrooms

Directions

The best way to teach fourth and fifth grade readers how to integrate and discuss comparative, contrasting, and integrative ideas between texts is to ask them to engage in a relatively simple and routine visual reading strategy. In short, when teaching a new or complex idea it is often helpful to build upon the students pre-existing schema.

For that reason, *Get Animated!: Teaching 21st Century Early Reader and Young Adult Cartoons Language Arts* suggests a familiar and simplistic reading strategy: the KWL chart. Because of its simple and clear three-column setup students will feel comfortable with the strategy, and, as hoped for, spend their critical thinking and decision-making time on the real task at hand, integrating and discussing knowledge and ideas between two different texts.

Because the **KWL** chart (**K**now—**W**onder—**L**earn) is structured into 3 three distinct, teachable moments the lesson plan that follows asks students to work through their reading of both the text and the cartoon on two separate handouts. Teachers can find blank, user-friendly handouts for this activity in Appendix F (remember each student needs two handouts, one for the cartoon and one for another text of your choice).

3. At this point, teachers will have two sets of 40 index cards, 80 cards total divided into four different categories for each text (cartoon and book).
4. Finally, teachers will have two clearly labeled visual centers. Opposite sides of the room would work best.
5. Each station should have a label: *Avatar* (or cartoon of choice) and *Walk Two Moons* (or print-text novel choice).
6. At each of the two stations place the corresponding four piles of index cards. For example, *Avatar* will have four piles: a plot pile of 10 index cards, a setting pile of 10 index cards, a characters pile of 10 index cards, and a favorite moment pile of 10 index cards. Fold a piece of paper or index card to make a label for each of the four categories at each station, placing the label (i.e., "plot") in front of its appropriate 10 index cards (10 plot index cards), and so on.

Figure 4.4 outlines the procedures for teaching this fun and exciting writing lesson plan integrating the elements of story from a cartoon with the elements of story from a print-text novel.

Teaching Reading with Children's Cartoons in Fourth and Fifth Grade 21st Century Language Arts Classrooms

Step 1

On the board or screen encourage students to share what they already **(K)**now about high-quality, memorable stories. Questions to spur on student schema about these elements of story could be:

- ▶ "In kindergarten through third grade you read many stories. What do you remember about these stories?"
- ▶ "Who are the people/living beings the story focuses on?"
- ▶ "What do we call where the story takes place?"
- ▶ "All of the events in the story make up the _(plot)_?"
- ▶ "Think about your favorite book. What makes it your all-time favorite?"

As students respond to these prompts (and other spontaneous questions that may arise) record their answers on both handouts in the **(K)**now column; students will want to reference both handouts later so it is indeed best to write down ideas on each handout.

While one handout is for the cartoon the second is for reading a second text.

Name: _____Text / Cartoon Title: _____&_____

(K)NOW (W)ONDER (L)EARN

_____

Plot

_____

Setting

_____

Characters

_____

Favorite Moments

(Continued)

Step 2

After a vibrant and fruitful discussion about these recognizable elements of story, ask students to view and analyze the cover of *Walk Two Moons* and the opening credits of the *Avatar* cartoon. Fifteen–thirty minutes per format.

▶ "Spend time viewing the cover of *Walk Two Moons* and write down what you **(W)**onder about the print-text book and its corresponding category (characters, setting, plot, etc.) on your first handout."
▶ "Next, spend time viewing the opening credits of *Avatar:* again, write down what you are **(W)**ondering alongside its corresponding **(W)**onder category on the second handout."

When students are finished writing down what they **(W)**onder about the cover of *Walk Two Moons* and the introductory credits of *Avatar* involve them in a discussion aimed at sharing ideas and building more and more questions to think about as they prepare to read each text and fill out the **(L)**earn column of their two KWL charts.

Step 3

The most significant portion of your classroom time will be spent reading the print-text novel.

In the case of *Walk Two Moons,* a more time-consuming chapter book, you may want to divide up the reading by offering students Silent Reading Time, Peer/Buddy reading time, and/or homework reading time. When they are done reading—or even as they read—students can use their *Walk Two Moons* handout to fill out the last column: What they are **(L)**earning from reading this text.

NOTE:
Because the cartoon episode is under 25 minutes teachers will want to wait and show it second, after students have read and completed their *Walk Two Moons* reading and handout.

For this particular lesson plan teachers and students can watch the first episode of *Avatar* entitled: *Avatar: Book One Water, Chapter One.* While watching this episode, teachers should encourage students to fill out their last **(L)**earn column on the second handout.

Last but not least, teachers and students need to share their thoughts and responses with each other—particularly from the **(L)**earned categories of their two **KWL** handouts.

Step 4

With their analysis and integration of how the two texts emphasize what students knew, wondered, and learned teachers can collect both handouts for assessments purposes.

Note: This is not a single lesson plan. *Get Animated!* recommends that teachers feel encouraged to consider pairing other texts with other literary-level cartoons throughout the year.

FIGURE 4.4
Writing-focused lesson plan integrating the teaching of cartoons with the teaching of print-text novels. Note: a generic, teacher-friendly version of this writing lesson plan can be found in Appendix G.

DIRECTIONS

There are two stations in the room.

- ▶ One station for *Avatar*.
- ▶ And one station for *Walk Two Moons*.

To start, you may choose which station you want to attend.

At each station you will find four sets of cards. Each set has a label, the same labels we used in the reading handouts you recently turned in: plot, setting, characters, favorite moments.

There are 10 cards for each labeled pile. Individually, **choose one card from two of the four piles found at your station.**

After you have your two cards, turn them over to see which character(s), setting(s), plot(s), or favorite moment(s) of your choice appear on the back.

Thinking about your two cards write a short story (with words and images) considering what would happen if these two cards were assigned to you as a writer of the next cartoon episode or book in the series. Blank paper, coloring and writing utensils can be found at each station.

You will have 40 minutes to brainstorm and outline your story.

After 40 minutes you will get into pairs and share your new story ideas with a friend. **While you take turns sharing and listening feel free to ask questions and make suggestions for your peer's story.**

Tomorrow (if there is not enough time today) you will take your drafted outlines and revise your new stories from brainstorms/outlines into a fully written story.

Finally, you will present your two index cards and the story you wrote to the entire class. When you are done sharing all of your hard work the class will ask questions and engage in a discussion about what they liked about your story.

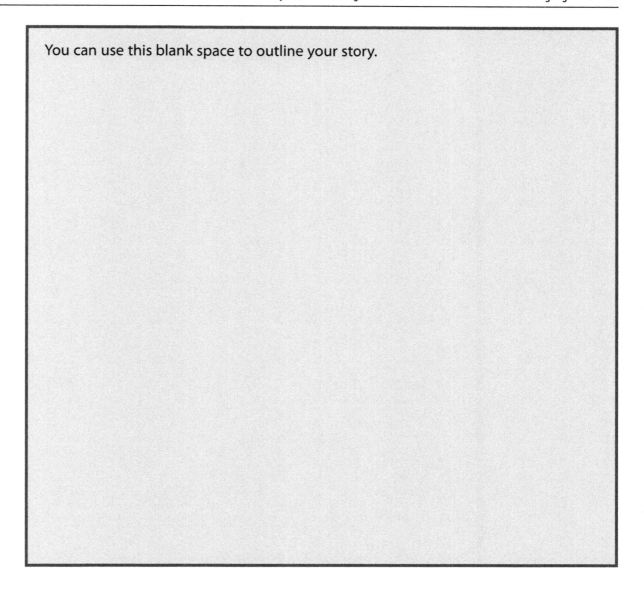

You can use this blank space to outline your story.

With a recommended reading and a recommended writing lesson plan for teaching 21st century cartoons in fourth and fifth grade Language Arts classrooms teachers and students have effectively addressed the Common Core Standards' (www.commoncore.org) emphasis on integrating various texts and purposes at both of these key grade levels. Furthermore, and in terms of assessment data, the writing lesson plan in this chapter can serve as evidence that students are not only readers of multi-literacies, but also writers of multi-literacies, the two most important skills they will need to survive in their future schooling, higher education, careers, and family lives.

One of the most important lessons history teaches us is that time never stops. Time keeps moving. For these key grade level readers—who are usually steered away from images (due to a more traditional perspective of teaching print-text literacies alone)—teachers can begin to shed that impression and embrace reading and writing with both images and words for these key grade level readers and writers in the 21st century.

Chapter 5

Teaching Young Adult Cartoons in 6th–8th Grade Language Arts

"Anyone interested in the world generally can't help being
interested in young adult culture—in the music, the bands,
the books, the fashions, and the way in which the young adult
community develops its own language."

Margaret Mahy, children's and young adult author

As an educator I am inclined to start this chapter by noting that the Language Arts Common Core Standards experience a grade level split between fifth and sixth grade. First, teachers will find the set of standards for teaching K–5 grade level Language Arts (as we noted in Chapters 1–4); second, teachers will find the set of standards for teaching 6–12 grade level Language Arts.

With the reader more in mind than the standard I feel inclined to call sensitive attention to something more important than this split: the shift between childhood and young adulthood reading and writing. Even though the standards for teaching Language Arts may be split in two grade level groupings, the best educators are those who first refer to their students' ability level before referring to their students' grade level suppose-abilities. As a former elementary and middle school Language Arts educator I often found (and still do) these middle level grade divisions challenging. While some of my middle level readers were indeed reading (and ready for!) young adult texts assigned to their literal grade level, some of their peers were not. My point: it is essential to reference students before standards. If our students are reading at or above a sixth grade level then by all means we should embrace those higher grade level standards discussed in the 6–12 Language Arts Common Core Standards, as we will in this chapter (see Figures 5.1, 5.2, and 5.3). If our students are not ready for this demarcating-split made by the Language Arts Common Core Standards (between fifth and sixth grades, between childhood reading and writing, between young adult reading and writing) it is our job to refer back to the earlier Language Arts Common Core Standards.

The line between children's cartoons and young adult cartoons can be just as thin as the line between middle and early grade level labels and standards. For that reason, this chapter of *Get Animated!* will help educators not only identify, but also teach middle level cartoons that span this sensitive age range. Please note that while some of these cartoons were referenced in earlier chapters they are referenced (and summarized) here for their more middle level reading and writing themes. Figure 5.1 lists and summarizes the best and most current cartoons that span this age range.

FIGURE 5.1
Young adult cartoons for teaching the transition between early level and middle level Language Arts Common Core Standards.

Cartoon and Channel	Brief Description
The Legend of Korra Nickelodeon	Linked to the themes and origins that surround the *Avatar* cartoon series, *The Legend of Korra* tells the story of a young girl who must maintain the balance restored to Republic City by Avatar Aang and Fire Lord Zuko to end the Hundred Years War. Whether spiritually inspired by their natural abilities to be a fire, water, earth, and/or air "Bender" residents of the city now live in peace. Sometimes that peace, however, is tested. It's up to our new air bender Korra to figure out a solution.
MAD Cartoon Network	Just like the older, magazine-inspired MAD cartoons and propaganda, this series spoofs everything about popular culture. Appropriate for young adults, this series is fun and engaging because it calls on young adults to react to and poke fun at their existing schema and real-world lives both in and out of school.
Invader Zim Nickelodeon	As mentioned in Chapter 4, this series does indeed maintain its status as one of the best cartoons of the 21st century. Intended for a young adult viewership Invader Zim is like any other alien character, right? He's out to take over the world! That's what Zim thinks, and he'll tell you too. It's not necessarily what his leaders or his earthly nemesis Dib think about the situation. Zim is a terrible and clumsy alien who trips all over what he thinks are his brilliant plans to destroy the world. Witty and sharp, Zim and his hilarious sidekick Gir maintain a loyal following.

FIGURE 5.1
Continued.

Cartoon and Channel	Brief Description
The Simpsons FOX	The most popular animated show ever, *The Simpsons* stars America's favorite family, in their favorite city (which indeed, the writers tease the viewer, can be found in the state of their choice). With themes like family, school, friendship, life-lessons, adventure, and misadventures *The Simpsons* repertoire of hit episodes is deep and more than ready for classroom literary exploration.
Bob's Burgers FOX	One of Fox's newest hit cartoon shows, *Bob's Burgers* stars a family of five, three children and their mom and dad. Bob and Louise own a burger joint, and Bob deems himself the best burger maker in the world. And even though the reader longs to agree with Bob—or at least find out—the family's misadventures are sometimes more intriguing.
The Clone Wars Cartoon Network	This series follows a young Anakin Skywalker as he trains to become a Master Jedi Knight under the guidance of Obi Wan Kenobi.
Futurama Comedy Central	Set in the future, this series stars a motley crew of characters as they work for a quirky and extremely old professor who owns a shipping and delivery business. As simple as their job may sound, however, the crew's various personalities manage to find trouble everywhere they go.
Adventure Time Cartoon Network	My best advice about Adventure Time is to watch it more than once. Although it may seem a bit distant and outlandish, this cartoon series is one of the best of its generation in terms of storytelling. Set in "The Land of Ooo" this series follows adventurers Finn and Jake as they set out to be heroes. With a supporting cast of very interesting co-stars and a lot of mythologically-based backstories viewers will soon become a part of this cartoon's loyal legions of fans.
Ultimate Spiderman Disney	Created by the always ingenious minds at Man of Action today's young readers get an all-new look at Peter Parker and Spiderman. Talking to the reader as if he or she were his diary, Peter Parker narrates his adventures in this all-new series. Complete with 21st century gadgets, lingo, and themes readers and teachers will both be able to explore how Spiderman presents himself to 21st century viewers.

FIGURE 5.1
Continued.

Cartoon and Channel	Brief Description
Gravity Falls Disney	Clever and endearing, the two main characters in this cartoon are forced to spend their summer with their awkwardly weird uncle, "Grumple Stan," who owns The Mystery Shack. A tourist-trap stocked full of Gravity Falls' most eccentric oddities and unexplainable finds Grumple Stan is a thought-provoking character the children come to adore. And that's where their adventures begin.

Adventure Time is an extremely popular cartoon that tends to span age and grade level labels. In fact, it has a very healthy, loyal, and devote adult viewership as well. Because it is ageless (and so very, very popular) this chapter of *Get Animated!* will detail how middle level Language Arts educators can teach reading and writing with its wealth of literary potential.

First, Figure 5.2 aligns the 6–12 Language Arts Common Core standards to a Guided Reading lesson plan for teaching the cartoon *Adventure Time* in middle level Language Arts classrooms. As in earlier chapters, a blank, teacher-friendly, and cartoon-choice adaptable version of this Guided Reading lesson plan can be found in Appendix H.

FIGURE 5.2
Common Core Standard Aligned and Guided Reading-focused Language Arts lesson plan for teaching *Adventure Time* in grades six and above.

Language Arts Common Core Standard Alignment for Grades Six and Above

Reading Key Ideas and Details

1. Read closely to determine what the text says explicitly and to make logical inferences from it; cite specific textual evidence when writing or speaking to support conclusions drawn from the text.
2. Determine central ideas or themes of a text and analyze their development; summarize the key supporting details and ideas.
3. Analyze how and why individuals, events, and ideas develop and interact over the course of a text.

Guided Reading Lesson Plan for Teaching *Adventure Time* in Sixth Grade Language Arts and Above

Materials: extra paper, writing utensils, character cards, setting cards, blank balloon cards, poster board(s) or large display paper(s) (for story-boarding)

Theme Words Written on the Board: friendship, romance, rivals, family

Character cards: various printed/drawn images of all the main characters in the story

Setting cards: various printed/drawn images of all the key settings in the story

Blank Balloon cards: various printed/drawn images of thought balloons, word balloons, idea balloons, and so on (teachers can find thousands of blank balloons by google searching "comic book balloons" as an image search).*

*Note: Teachers will want to preview the episode they wish to have students read, and pick out the key moments that involve inference or insinuation of key ideas and details for the characters, settings, and words and images appropriate for the cards they will make.

In regard to *Adventure Time* and teaching middle level reading I recommend an episode that features Finn, Jake, the Ice King, the Flame Princess, Marceline, and Princess Bubblegum.

Before Reading

To start, ask students to share their thoughts on the four themes written on the board: friendship, romance, rivals, family. If students need help building schema about any of these words teachers can pass out dictionaries or grant access to dictionary Internet access.

Next, teachers can introduce students to, and pass out, the various cards affiliated with the characters and settings in their chosen *Adventure Time* episode. Every small group of 3–4 students will need their own set of character and setting cards.

Looking at the character cards and setting cards ask students:
"Look at and discuss your character and setting cards. After looking at the cards, reflect upon our four themes (friends, romance, rivals, family) and try to predict how each of these four themes might be related to the key ideas and/or details in this episode of *Adventure Time* And why?"

Teachers can make two columns on the board: characters and setting. In those two columns record students' predictions and responses. Educators can also feel free to build schema for students by giving them hints about their ideas and the various cards. All of these ideas should be on the board for student reference.

During Reading

As students view/read the episode in small groups ask them to discuss their comprehension as they go (feeling free to pause the episode at key moments). Specifically, students need to follow along and place the character and setting cards in the correct order on their display paper. Prompt students to: "Choose and place the appropriate character and setting cards in the order they appear in the story. Between each card write down one or more of the four themes (main ideas or key details) that best describe the connection between cards. After reading this episode of *Adventure Time* be ready to explain your decisions to the entire class."

After Reading

When students are finished reading your selected *Adventure Time* episode, offer them the five prepared blank balloon cards.

Ask students to create and arrange their characters cards, setting cards, and blank balloon cards in order to make the themes or main ideas and key details even more obvious.

On a second sheet/the reverse side of their previous display board offer students the following directions:

► "Use your new, five blank balloon cards to fill in any gaps in the story that you feel exists between your character and setting cards. Try to pay extra attention to further highlighting the four themes or key ideas and details from the story: friendship, romance, rivals, family."

When everyone is finished we will share and discuss our final thoughts and additions about the episode and your thematic enhancements.

Because the guided reading lesson plan found in Figure 5.2 is focused on student comprehension of the story, with an added twist of additional story elements determined by the students' balloon cards, the writing lesson plan will call on students to further their cartoon composition ideas with *Adventure Time*. Figure 5.3 lists the Common Core Standards that align to teaching the previously (or a new) episode of *Adventure Time*.

FIGURE 5.3
Common Core Standard alignment for teaching writing with
middle level children's cartoons (Appendix I).

Common Core Standard Alignment for Teaching Writing with Cartoons for Young Adults

Production and Distribution of Writing

1. Produce clear and coherent writing in which the development, organization, and style are appropriate to task, purpose, and audience.
2. Develop and strengthen writing as needed by planning, revising, editing, rewriting, or trying a new approach.
3. Use technology, including the Internet, to produce and publish writing and to interact and collaborate with others.

To teach students to writing their own middle level or young adult cartoons, teachers need to plan a two-stage process:

▶ Stage 1: Content and Clarity
▶ Stage 2: The Writing Process

The following writing lesson plan for middle level writers of cartoons will provide specific details for each of the stages (Figure 5.4).

FIGURE 5.4
Language Arts lesson plan for teaching writing with young adult cartoons.
A blank, user-friendly version for teachers can be found in Appendix I.

Language Arts Lesson Plan for Teaching Writing with Young Adult Cartoons

Materials needed for this lesson: scrap paper, small index cards, large poster/display boards, writing utensils (all colors). Various images of characters, settings, and primary plot points; for this writing-focused lesson plan students can also feel free to write their own graphic novel without these cut-outs, drawing on their own, if they wish.

Directions (2 options):

Option 1: If teachers would like to build upon the episode of *Adventure Time* students have already seen, they can begin this lesson by asking students to review and reflect upon their previously completed Guided Reading lesson plan.

Option 2: If teachers would like to add more schema to their students' understanding of *Adventure Time* they can show a second, thematically complimentary episode. Students may also want to reference their previous Guided Reading lesson plan as well.

Step 1: Task
Inform students that their first **TASK** will be to reflect upon the previously seen episode(s) of *Adventure Time* and review their newly completed Guided Reading lesson plan. Students can have anywhere from 10–20 minutes to discuss the most memorable moments from the cartoon(s) and the Guided Reading lesson plan.

With this schema-based discussion about the characters, plot, and setting in place, teachers can inform students that their next **TASK** (and feel free to write these directions on the board) will be to add an entirely new theme/main idea to the story. In order to demonstrate and combine their reading comprehension and their own original ideas as writers have them:

"Given what you know about the characters, plot, and setting your writing **TASK** is to add an entirely new theme, main idea, character, or setting to the story. Individually or in small groups use some scrap paper to brainstorm some ideas" (20–30 minutes).

Step 2: Purpose and Audience (teachers can share/write directions on the board)

PURPOSE: "Once you select your favorite brainstormed idea start planning and thinking about how your new idea would influence and fit into the episode(s) and themes we discussed as you read the cartoon (and completed your Guided Reading lesson plan). In order to simulate the movement and visual nature of cartoons, blank index cards will be provided. Each index card represents a snapshot of your new story idea.

FIGURE 5.4
Continued.

Be sure to glue/tape index cards in order on your new sheet of poster or display paper. You are encouraged to use words and images to represent your ideas for each snapshot."

Remember: You will be sharing your new ideas and additions for the cartoon with the class. Be sure to put your index cards in order: from top to bottom and left to right. Professional animators refer to this process as "storyboarding."

Audience: You are writing your episode for someone who has NOT seen the show.

At the beginning of this chapter you found a quotation from the famous children's and young adult author Margaret Mahy, reminding you that in order to genuinely teach young adult readers you must immerse yourself in their cultural, real-world realities. The question is not: How can I get my young readers to better understand my curriculum? The question is: How can I align my curriculum to my young readers and their realities?

By acknowledging and valuing the cartoons that populate and animate the thoughts and imaginations of today's young adult minds educators can prepare them for the reading and writing they will actually do in their soon-to-be-adult lives, and it just so happens that it is during this time in history we redefine reading to mean viewing both visually and verbally—like in cartoons.

Appendix A

Guided reading lesson plan for teaching children's cartoons in K–1st grade Language Arts classrooms

---

YOU WILL NEED THE FOLLOWING MATERIALS FOR THIS LESSON PLAN:

- ► projection screen/television
- ► the cartoon episode of your choice, which can be found online through the network's cartoon listings, or online at youtube.com
- ► blank paper
- ► crayons, markers, pencils, colored pencils, and pens

COMMON CORE STANDARD ALIGNMENT

Key Ideas and Details

1. Read closely to determine what the text says explicitly and to make logical inferences from it; cite specific textual evidence when writing or speaking to support conclusions drawn from the text.
2. Determine central ideas or themes of a text and analyze their development; summarize the key supporting details and ideas.
3. Analyze how and why individuals, events, and ideas develop and interact over the course of a text.

Before Reading

Arthur—Season: 16—Episode: 5b—"Read and Flumberghast"

http://www.youtube.com/watch?v=_818bVDw038

Before reading ask students what they **KNOW** either about _____ (series/ episode) and/or the idea of _____ (a theme from your selection). Next, ask students what they **WONDER** either about _____ or _____. On the board, record their responses in the appropriate **KNOW-and-WONDER** categories.

KNOW   **WONDER**

During Reading

As students read and view this episode about Arthur and imagination, pause the episode at least three times. During each pause ask students what they have **LEARNED** about Arthur and his friends. On the board teachers can visually emphasize and honor student responses by adding, and keeping notes on a third category of discussion (**LEARN**).

KNOW   **WONDER**   **LEARN**

After Reading

When students are done viewing and reading, it's time to check-in on their overall comprehension of this particular episode. To do so, teachers can ask their students to be cartoonists themselves. Allow students to choose one of the following two writing prompts; I recommend reading these prompts aloud (or visually posting) due to the early grade level of these students.

"On your paper, draw a picture of your **favorite Arthur character**. What does this character look like? What do we know about him or her? How does what you drew reflect this character's personality? After you finish drawing be ready to share your drawing with the class."

or

"On your paper, write down some words or images that help you remember the most important **character or characters** from this episode."

APPENDIX B

Common Core Standard-Aligned Lesson Plan for Teaching Writing With K–1st Grade Children's Cartoons

YOU WILL NEED THE FOLLOWING MATERIALS FOR THIS LESSON PLAN:

▶ A large cut-out image of ___main character___
▶ A visual space where you can post and display _large cut-out of main characters_ for all students to see
▶ Chalk, markers, or other writing utensils for listing student ideas about this episode

COMMON CORE STANDARD ALIGNMENT

Text Types and Purposes

1. Write arguments to support claims in an analysis of substantive topics or texts, using valid reasoning and relevant and sufficient evidence.
2. Write informative/explanatory texts to examine and convey complex ideas and information clearly and accurately through the effective selection, organization, and analysis of content.
3. Write narratives to develop real or imagined experiences or events using effective technique, well-chosen details, and well-structured event sequences.

Directions

Before watching an episode of _____ display a large cut-out image of _____ (main character/s) for all students to see. In order to build upon their already existing or new schema, ask students to share what they already know about _____. Draw images or write words to represent all of the various ideas students have about _____.

Next, tell students: "As we watch this episode of _____ pretend you are a detective. A detective looks for clues about people, places, and/or ideas. When you are done watching the episode, we will discuss what you find, **and write** about the story."

Before you finally turn on the episode ask students if they have any questions. Then, play the selected episode of _____.

When the episode is over write the three or four key context clue words from the directions on the board, near the image of _____: "_____", "_____," "_____," and "_____." Remind students about the definitions for each key word.

After reminding them about each word, ask students to recall—with words and images—what they learned from watching this episode, especially in terms of the key words you listed from the story. Discuss the student's writing and/or drawing suggestions as you move from one response to the next response.

APPENDIX C

A Carousel Reading Lesson Plan for Teaching the Common Core Standard's Emphasis on Craft and Structure in Second and Third Grade Language Arts Classrooms

---

Three-Step Reading Carousel Activity for Teaching The Common Core Standards' Focus on Craft and Structure in Second and Third Grade Language Arts with _____

Step 1: Schema Building

Before students enter the classroom and are ready to start their day post five stations around the room: labeled "character(s)," "setting(s)," "plot(s)," "theme(s)," and point of view(s)." In case students need some help building schema about any of these structural and craft-oriented terms please feel free to add helpful definitions below their labels.

As they enter the classroom inform them that they will be rotating like a carousel—clockwise—in small groups of three to five.

In small groups ask students to report to one of the five stations displayed throughout the room.

The directions on the board should read: "There are five stations around the room. We will work through the stations two different times, **once before reading and once after reading.**

To start, we will activate our schema about some key terms found in crafting high-quality stories, emphasizing important components such as character(s), setting(s), plot(s), theme(s), and point of view(s)."

Teacher Notes: Please be sure to put your station-postings around the room on large, visible paper. For upcoming student usage you will also want to leave a few writing utensils at each station as well.

Your next set of directions for students should read like this: "Each station is labeled and contains a critical element of story term. And even though I have provided you with brief definitions please use the markers at each station to come up with your own ideas/your own words to define each term during our first carousel session. You can write your ideas directly on the poster board."

After giving each group 10 minutes at each station, take the poster boards down and bring them to the front of the room, for a full classroom discussion of what each group wrote down for each term.

(Continued)

Step 2: Empowering Students to Know the Significant 21st Century Literacies of Their Own Time and Place in History

Before completing step number 2, educators will want to show their students an episode of _____. That said, and from someone who adores children and is a fan of the show herself, any episode you select will be of high quality.

Before turning the episode on remind students that:

"You are the first, most unique and exciting generation to ever experience the vast amount of changes currently happening all around the world in regard to reading and writing; indeed, you are the very first students to set the stage for reading and writing with multiple literacies for generations to come. That's a pretty awesome superhero responsibility. Right now—today—is an opportunity to make a significant and critical difference in not only the future of reading for yourselves, but also the future of reading for your own future children.

Capable of determining what it means to read from instantaneous access to a variety of screen-like and image-dominant 21st century platforms, your generation reads multiple literacies every day: especially from RPG and educational videogames, iPads, iPhones, text messaging, Skype, internet, and emails, you are in written and visual contact with anyone in the world at any time of day or night."

With their empowered and special hero-like qualities at the forefront as motivation, it is now time to watch the selected episode of _____.

Step 3: Building a New Literacy Bridge

Because our students are living during a critical time in history, and we are teaching them during that time (an age-level when previous generations of our colleagues have been encouraged to steer children away from visuals and toward an emphasis on print-text literacies alone) this third step is critical to teaching a shared literacy stage with two actors upon it: image text and verbal text.

For that reason, the third step in this reading lesson for second and third grade readers of children's cartoons asks students to think about both the visuals and the words that inform each of the previously mentioned crafted elements of story: plot, character, theme, setting, and point of view.

As they read the episode ask students to complete the following worksheet.

Directions: To the right of each character, list or draw the words and the images that give this character his/her unique perspective about what happens in this episode.

	Words	/	Images
Character 1			
Character 2			
Character 3			
Character 4			
Character 5			

APPENDIX D

Directions and Common Core Standard Alignment for Teaching Second and Third Grade Students to Write Their Own _____ Episode

---

COMMON CORE STANDARD ALIGNMENT FOR TEACHING WRITING WITH CARTOONS IN SECOND AND THIRD GRADE LANGUAGE ARTS CLASSROOMS

Text Types and Purposes

1. Write arguments to support claims in an analysis of substantive topics or texts, using valid reasoning and relevant and sufficient evidence.
2. Write informative/explanatory texts to examine and convey complex ideas and information clearly and accurately through the effective selection, organization, and analysis of content.
3. Write narratives to develop real or imagined experiences or events using effective technique, well-chosen details, and well-structured event sequences.

DIRECTIONS

Step 1:

With your group members, report to one of the carousel stations around the room. One group per station.

Step 2:

Once at your station take note of the category you will be focusing on and review the work the class recently completed about that particular category during the reading lesson plan.

Step 3:

Please note that another, second blank piece of poster paper is also now hanging at this station, complete with the corresponding categorical label.

Step 4:

After reviewing the reading lesson plan work you previously engaged in for each category discuss some new ideas centered on your assigned category. For example, if your category is "plot" brainstorm some new "plot" ideas for a potential, future episode of _____.

Your new ideas need to focus on two criteria:

1. A realistic portrayal of what we learned about your category given the previous episode. The "theme" group, for instance, will want to make sure that their ideas about the themes are accurate and reflective of what we already know, and
2. Strong emphasis on further developing your assigned category as the main subject for a new story idea (for instance, the characters group will want to center their new episode ideas on character development).

Continued.

Step 5:

With your group's categorical emphasis at the center of your discussion work together to write your own episode of _____. You will have between 30 and 45 minutes to outline or write out your ideas.

Step 6:

Present your ideas to the rest of the class in the following order:

1. Identify your category.
2. Share your new episode idea, particularly how you will further explore your assigned category.
3. Explain and answer peer's questions about how your new idea emphasizes the category you were assigned and a further, growing knowledge of a character(s).

Potential Starter-Questions to Ask Each Group:

► "Why did you decide to . . .?"
► "What was your goal in choosing to . . .?"
► "Who came up with the idea to _____, and how did the idea build?"
► "How did your group work together to reach the decision to . . .?"

APPENDIX E

Common Core Standard Alignment for a Supplemental, Extra Writing Activity Regarding Teaching _____ in Second and Third Grade Language Arts

---

Built upon the reading lesson plan for second and third grade Language Arts.

> **Production and Distribution of Writing**
>
> 1. Produce clear and coherent writing in which the development, organization, and style are appropriate to task, purpose, and audience.

When students have completed writing their own new episodes of _____ teachers may want to offer them extra time to act out their new episode idea. Like Reader's Theatre, students would engage in a second writing stage that asks them to focus on the next set of key Common Core Standards for writing in second and third grade Language Arts. Figure 3.6 highlights the Common Core Standards students would be working with if allowed time to complete this extra, supplemental writing activity focused on children's cartoons.

APPENDIX F

Teaching Reading with Children's Cartoons In 21st Century Fourth and Fifth Grade Language Arts Classrooms

---

Common Core Standard Alignment for Teaching Children's Cartoons in Fourth and Fifth Grade Language Arts Classrooms
Integration of Knowledge and Ideas   1. Integrate and evaluate content presented in diverse media and formats, including visually and quantitatively, as well as in words.   2. Delineate and evaluate the argument and specific claims in a text, including the validity of the reasoning as well as the relevance and sufficiency of the evidence.   3. Analyze how two or more texts address similar themes or topics in order to build knowledge or to compare the approaches the authors take.

Even though these are some of the more advanced Common Core Standards for teaching reading in K–5 classrooms, pairing an animated cartoon with a print-text book is a perfect and simple solution. In regard to pairing, *Get Animated!: Teaching 21st Century Early Reader and Young Adult Cartoons Language Arts* recommends one of two possible pairings when teaching Elementary Language Arts with _____ cartoon episode:

1. Due to its popularity teachers can easily find both print-text books and/or graphic novels to pair with the _____ cartoon.
2. Due to its timelessness and high quality storytelling teachers can also easily choose a more traditional fourth or fifth grade print-text book to pair with _____.

Teaching Reading with Children's Cartoons in Fourth and Fifth Grade 21st Century Language Arts Classrooms

Directions

The best way to teach fourth and fifth grade readers how to integrate and discuss comparative, contrasting, and integrative ideas between texts is to ask them to engage in a relatively simple and routine visual reading strategy. In short, when teaching a new or complex idea it is often helpful to build upon the students pre-existing schema.

For that reason, *Get Animated!: Teaching 21st Century Early Reader and Young Adult Cartoons Language Arts* suggests a familiar and simplistic reading strategy: the KWL chart. Because of its simple and clear three-column setup students will feel comfortable with the strategy, and, as hoped for, spend their critical thinking and decision-making time on the real task at hand, integrating and discussing knowledge and ideas between two different texts.

Because the **KWL** chart (**K**now—**W**onder—**L**earn) is structured into 3 three distinct, teachable moments the lesson plan that follows asks students to work through their reading of both the text and the cartoon on two separate handouts. Teachers can find blank, user-friendly handouts for this activity in Appendix F (remember each student needs two handouts, one for the cartoon and one for another text of your choice).

Teaching Reading with Children's Cartoons in Fourth and Fifth Grade 21st Century Language Arts Classrooms

Step 1

On the board or screen encourage students to share what they already **(K)**now about high-quality, memorable stories. Questions to spur on student schema about these elements of story could be:

▶ "In kindergarten through third grade you read many stories. What do you remember about these stories?"
▶ "Who are the people/living beings the story focuses on?"
▶ "What do we call where the story takes place?"
▶ "All of the events in the story make up the ___(plot)___?"
▶ "Think about your favorite book. What makes it your all-time favorite?"

As students respond to these prompts (and other spontaneous questions that may arise) record their answers on both handouts in the **(K)**now column; students will want to reference both handouts later so it is indeed best to write down ideas on each handout.

While one handout is for the cartoon the second is for reading a second text.

Name: _____ Text / Cartoon Title: _____ & _____

(K)NOW (W)ONDER (L)EARN

_____
Plot

_____
Setting

_____
Characters

_____
Favorite Moments

(Continued)

Step 2

After a vibrant and fruitful discussion about these recognizable elements of story, ask students to view and analyze the cover of *Walk Two Moons* and the opening credits of the *Avatar* cartoon. Fifteen–thirty minutes per format.

▶ "Spend time viewing the cover of *Walk Two Moons* and write down what you (**W**)onder about the print-text book and its corresponding category (characters, setting, plot, etc.) on your first handout."

▶ "Next, spend time viewing the opening credits of *Avatar*: again, write down what you are (**W**)ondering alongside its corresponding (**W**)onder category on the second handout."

When students are finished writing down what they (**W**)onder about the cover of *Walk Two Moons* and the introductory credits of *Avatar* involve them in a discussion aimed at sharing ideas and building more and more questions to think about as they prepare to read each text and fill out the (**L**)earn column of their two KWL charts.

Step 3

The most significant portion of your classroom time will be spent reading the print-text novel.

In the case of *Walk Two Moons,* a more time-consuming chapter book, you may want to divide up the reading by offering students Silent Reading Time, Peer/Buddy reading time, and/or homework reading time. When they are done reading—or even as they read—students can use their *Walk Two Moons* handout to fill out the last column: What they are (**L**)earning from reading this text.

NOTE:
Because the cartoon episode is under 25 minutes teachers will want to wait and show it second, after students have read and completed their *Walk Two Moons* reading and handout.

For this particular lesson plan teachers and students can watch the first episode of *Avatar* entitled: *Avatar: Book One Water, Chapter One.* While watching this episode, teachers should encourage students to fill out their last (**L**)**earn** column on the second handout.

Last but not least, teachers and students need to share their thoughts and responses with each other—particularly from the (**L**)earned categories of their two **KWL** handouts.

Step 4

With their analysis and integration of how the two texts emphasize what students knew, wondered, and learned teachers can collect both handouts for assessments purposes.

Note: This is not a single lesson plan. *Get Animated!* recommends that teachers feel encouraged to consider pairing other texts with other literary-level cartoons throughout the year.

APPENDIX G

Writing-Focused Lesson Plan Integrating the Teaching of Cartoons with the Teaching of Print-Text Novels in Fourth and Fifth Grade Language Arts

DIRECTIONS

There are two stations in the room.

▶ One station for _____ .
▶ And one station for _____ .

To start, you may choose which station you want to attend.

At each station you will find four sets of cards. Each set has a label, the same labels we used in the reading handouts you recently turned in: plot, setting, characters, favorite moments.

There are 10 cards for each labeled pile. Individually, **choose one card from two of the four piles found at your station.**

After you have your two cards, turn them over to see which character(s), setting(s), plot(s), or favorite moment(s) of your choice appear on the back.

Thinking about your two cards write a short story (with words and images) considering what would happen if these two cards were assigned to you as a writer of the next cartoon episode or book in the series. Blank paper, coloring and writing utensils can be found at each station.

You will have 40 minutes to brainstorm and outline your story.

After 40 minutes you will get into pairs and share your new story ideas with a friend. **While you take turns sharing and listening feel free to ask questions and make suggestions for your peer's story.**

Tomorrow (if there is not enough time today) you will take your drafted outlines and revise your new stories from brainstorms/outlines into a fully written story.

Finally, you will present your two index cards and the story you wrote to the entire class. When you are done sharing all of your hard work the class will ask questions and engage in a discussion about what they liked about your story.

You can use this blank space to outline your story.

APPENDIX H

Common Core Standard Aligned and Guided Reading-Focused Language Arts Lesson Plan for Teaching Adventure Time in Grades Six and Above

Language Arts Common Core Standard Alignment for Grades Six and Above
Reading Key Ideas and Details 1. Read closely to determine what the text says explicitly and to make logical inferences from it; cite specific textual evidence when writing or speaking to support conclusions drawn from the text. 2. Determine central ideas or themes of a text and analyze their development; summarize the key supporting details and ideas. 3. Analyze how and why individuals, events, and ideas develop and interact over the course of a text.

Guided Reading Lesson Plan for Teaching *Adventure Time* in Sixth Grade Language Arts and Above

Materials: extra paper, writing utensils, character cards, setting cards, blank balloon cards, poster board(s) or large display paper(s) (for story-boarding)

Theme Words Written on the Board: _____, _____, _____, and _____

Character cards: various printed/drawn images of all the main characters in the story

Setting cards: various printed/drawn images of all the key settings in the story

Blank Balloon cards: various printed/drawn images of thought balloons, word balloons, idea balloons, and so on (teachers can find thousands of blank balloons by google searching "comic book balloons" as an image search).*

*Note: Teachers will want to preview the episode they wish to have students read, and pick out the key moments that involve inference or insinuation of key ideas and details for the characters, settings, and words and images appropriate for the cards they will make.

Before Reading

To start, ask students to share their thoughts on the four themes written on the board: _____, _____, _____, and _____. If students need help building schema about any of these words teachers can pass out dictionaries or grant access to dictionary Internet access.

Next, teachers can introduce students to, and pass out, the various cards affiliated with the characters and settings in their chosen _____ episode. Every small group of 3–4 students will need their own set of character and setting cards.

Looking at the character cards and setting cards ask students:
"Look at and discuss your character and setting cards. After looking at the cards, reflect upon our four themes (_____, _____, _____, and _____) and try to predict how each of these four themes might be related to the key ideas and/or details in this episode of _____. And why?"

Teachers can make two columns on the board: characters and setting. In those two columns record students' predictions and responses. Educators can also feel free to build schema for students by giving them hints about their ideas and the various cards. All of these ideas should be on the board for student reference.

During Reading

As students view/read the episode in small groups ask them to discuss their comprehension as they go (feeling free to pause the episode at key moments). Specifically, students need to follow along and place the character and setting cards in the correct order on their display paper. Prompt students to: "Choose and place the appropriate character and setting cards in the order they appear in the story. Between each card write down one or more of the four themes (main ideas or key details) that best describe the connection between cards. After reading this episode of _____ be ready to explain your decisions to the entire class."

After Reading

When students are finished reading your selected _____ episode, offer them the five prepared blank balloon cards.

Ask students to create and arrange their characters cards, setting cards, and blank balloon cards in order to make the themes or main ideas and key details even more obvious.

On a second sheet/the reverse side of their previous display board offer students the following directions:

▶ "Use your new, five blank balloon cards to fill in any gaps in the story that you feel exists between your character and setting cards. Try to pay extra attention to further highlighting the four themes or key ideas and details from the story: _____, _____, _____, and _____."

When everyone is finished we will share and discuss our final thoughts and additions about the episode and your thematic enhancements.

APPENDIX I

Common Core Standard-Aligned Language Arts Lesson Plan for Teaching Writing with Young Adult Cartoons in Sixth Grade and Above

---

Common Core Standard Alignment for Teaching Writing with Cartoons for Young Adults
Production and Distribution of Writing   1. Produce clear and coherent writing in which the development, organization, and style are appropriate to task, purpose, and audience.   2. Develop and strengthen writing as needed by planning, revising, editing, rewriting, or trying a new approach.   3. Use technology, including the Internet, to produce and publish writing and to interact and collaborate with others.

Language Arts Lesson Plan for Teaching Writing with Young Adult Cartoons

Materials needed for this lesson: scrap paper, small index cards, large poster/display boards, writing utensils (all colors). Various images of characters, settings, and primary plot points; for this writing-focused lesson plan students can also feel free to write their own graphic novel without these cut-outs, drawing on their own, if they wish.

Directions (2 options):

Option 1: If teachers would like to build upon the episode of _____ students have already seen, they can begin this lesson by asking students to review and reflect upon their previously completed Guided Reading lesson plan.

Option 2: If teachers would like to add more schema to their students' understanding of _____ they can show a second, thematically complimentary episode. Students may also want to reference their previous Guided Reading lesson plan as well.

Step 1: Task
Inform students that their first **TASK** will be to reflect upon the previously seen episode(s) of _____ and review their newly completed Guided Reading lesson plan. Students can have anywhere from 10–20 minutes to discuss the most memorable moments from the cartoon(s) and the Guided Reading lesson plan.

With this schema-based discussion about the characters, plot, and setting in place, teachers can next inform students that their next **TASK** (and feel free to write these directions on the board) will be to add an entirely new theme/main idea to the story. In order to demonstrate and combine their reading comprehension and their own original ideas as writers have them:

"Given what you know about the characters, plot, and setting your writing **TASK** is to add an entirely new theme, main idea, character, or setting to the story. Individually or in small groups use some scrap paper to brainstorm some ideas" (20–30 minutes).

Step 2: Purpose and Audience (teachers can share/write directions on the board)

PURPOSE: "Once you select your favorite brainstormed idea start planning and thinking about how your new idea would influence and fit into the episode(s) and themes we discussed as you read the cartoon (and completed your Guided Reading lesson plan). In order to simulate the movement and visual nature of cartoons, blank index cards will be provided. Each index card represents a snapshot of your new story idea. Be sure to glue/tape index cards in order on your new sheet of poster or display paper. You are encouraged to use words and images to represent your ideas for each snapshot."

Remember: You will be sharing your new ideas and additions for the cartoon with the class. Be sure to put your index cards in order: from top to bottom and left to right. Professional animators refer to this process as "storyboarding."

Audience: You are writing your episode for someone who has NOT seen the show.

Bibliography

Buckingham, D. (2003). *Media education: Literacy, learning and contemporary culture.* Malden, MA: Polity.

Fountas, I., & Pinnell, G. (1996). *Teaching for comprehending and fluency: Thinking, talking, and writing about reading, K–8.* Portsmouth, NH: Heinemann.

Gardner, H. (1983). *Frames of mind: The theory of multiple intelligences.* New York: Basic Books.

Gee, J. P. (2003). *What video games have to teach us about learning and literacy.* New York: Palgrave.

Henderson, J. G., & Gornik, R. (2007). *Transformative curriculum leadership.* Upper Saddle River, NJ: Pearson.

Hobbs, R. (1998). The Simpsons meet Mark Twain: Analyzing popular media in the classroom. *The English Journal,* 87(1), 49–51.

Hobbs, R. (2007). *Reading the media: Media literacy in high school English.* New York: Teachers College Press.

Hull, G., & Schultz, K. (2002). *School's out: Bridging out-of-school literacies with classroom practice.* New York: Teachers College Press.

Kist, W. (2004). *New literacies in action.* New York: Teachers College Press.

Kist, W. (2009). *The socially networked classroom.* Thousand Oaks, CA: Corwin.

Kress, G. (2003). *Literacy in the new media age.* New York: Routledge.

Monnin, K. (2010). *Teaching graphic novels.* Gainesville, FL: Maupin House.

Monnin, K. (2011). *Teaching early reader comic books and graphic novels.* Gainesville, FL: Maupin House.

Monnin, K. (2012). *Using Content-Area Graphic texts for learning.* Gainesville, FL: Maupin House.

Monnin, K. (2013). *Teaching reading comprehension with graphic texts.* Mankato, MN: Capstone.

Meyrowitz, J. (1985). *No sense of place: The impact of electronic media on social behavior.* New York: Oxford.

The New London Group. (1996). A pedagogy of multi-literacies: Designing social futures. Harvard Educational Review, 66(1), 60–92.

Additional Resources

Altheide, D. (1996). *Qualitative media analysis.* Thousand Oaks: Sage.

Altschuler, T. (1968). Using popular media to achieve traditional goals. College Composition and Communication, 19(5), 340–347.

Amelio, R. J. (1976). American genre film: Teaching popular movies. English Journal, 65(3), 47–50.

Applebee, A. (1974). *Tradition and reform in the teaching of English.* Urbana, IL: NCTE.

Appleman, D. (2000). *Critical encounters in high school English: Teaching literary theory to adolescents.* New York: Teachers College Press.

Clark, R. (1983). Reconsidering research on learning from media. Review of Educational Research, 53(4), 445–459.

Eisner, E. W. (1991). *The enlightened eye: Qualitative inquiry and the enhancement of educational practice.* New York: Macmillan.

Eisner, E. W. (1998). *The kind of schools we need: Personal essays.* Portsmouth, NH: Heinemann.

Eisner, W. (1985). *Comics and sequential art.* New York: Poorhouse Press.

Eisner, W. (1996). *Graphic storytelling.* New York: Poorhouse Press.

Fehlman, R. H. (1992). Making meanings visible: Critically reading TV. The English Journal, 81(7), 19–24.

Fish, S. (1980). *Is there a text in this class?* Cambridge: Harvard University Press.

Fiske, J. (2004). *Reading television.* New York: Routledge.

Fox, R. (2005). Researching media literacy: Pitfalls and possibilities. In G. Schwartz & P. U. Brown (Eds.), *Media literacy: Transforming curriculum and teaching* (pp. 251–259). Malden, MA: Blackwell.

Freire, P. (1968). *Pedagogy of the oppressed.* New York: Continuum.

Freire, P., & Giroux, H. (1989). Pedagogy, popular culture, and public life. In H. Giroux & R. Simon (Eds.), *Popular culture: Schooling and everyday life* (pp. vii–xii). New York: Bergin & Garvey.

Giroux, H., & Simon, R. (1989). Popular culture and pedagogy of pleasure and meaning. In H. Giroux & R. Simon (Eds.), *Popular culture: Schooling and everyday life* (pp. 1–30). New York: Bergin & Garvey.

Hart, A., & Benson, A. (1996). Researching media education in English classrooms in the UK. Journal of Educational Media, 22(1), 7–22.

Hatfield, W. (1935). *An experience curriculum in English.* Urbana, IL: NCTE.

Howell, W. J. (1973). Art versus entertainment in the mass media: (A model for classroom discussion). Education, 94(2), 177–181.

Jenkins, H. (2006). *Convergence culture: Where old and new media collide.* New York: New York University Press.

Johnson, S. (2005). *Everything bad is good for you.* New York, NY: Penguin.

Kliebard, H. (2004). *The struggle for the American curriculum: 1893–1958.* New York: Routledge.

Langer, J. (1998). Thinking and doing literature: An eight year study. English Journal, 87(2), 16–23.

Leavis, F. R., & Thompson, D. (1933). *Culture and environment: The training of critical awareness.* Portsmouth, NH: Greenwood.

Maloney, H. B. (1960). Stepsisters of print: The public arts in the high school English class. The English Journal, 49(8), 570–579.

Masterman, L. (1985). *Teaching the media.* New York: Routledge.

McBrien, J. L. (1999). New texts, new tools: An argument for media literacy. Educational Leadership, 57(2), 76–79.

Messaris, P. (1994). *Visual literacy: Image, mind, & reality.* Boulder, CO: Westview Press.

Morrell, E. (2004). *Linking literacy and popular culture.* Norwood, MA: Christopher-Gordon Publishers.

National Institute for Literacy. (1991). National literacy act of 1991 (102nd Congress-1st Session Publication No. 102-73). Washington, DC: US Government Printing Office.

Newsom Report. (1963). Half our future. London: HMSO.

Owen, D., Silet, C., & Brown, S. (1988, September). Teaching television to empower students. The English Journal, 87, 84–87.

Pool, I. (1983). *Technologies of freedom.* Cambridge, MA: Harvard University Press.

Purves, A., & Pradl, G. (2003). The school subject literature. In J. Flood, D. Lapp, J. Squire, & J. Jensen (Eds.), Handbook of research on teaching the English language arts (pp. 323–354). Mahweh, NJ: Lawrence Erlbaum.

Richards, I. A. (1929). *Principles of literary criticism.* New York: Routledge.

Rosenblatt, L. (1938). *The reader, the text, the poem: The transactional theory of the literary work.* Carbondale, IL: Southern Illinois University Press.

Shor, I. (1980). *Critical teaching and everyday life.* Chicago: University of Chicago Press.

Smith, D. (1952). The English Language Arts. Urbana, IL: NCTE.

CPSIA information can be obtained at www.ICGtesting.com
Printed in the USA
LVOW02s0626020715

444319LV00004B/8/P

9 781465 231970